THE HEALTH POLICY AGENDA

Some Critical Questions

THE
HEALTH Some
POLICY Critical
Questions
AGENDA

Marion Ein Lewin, editor

American Enterprise Institute for Public Policy Research
Washington, D.C.

I thank the Pew Memorial trust for its support of the seminars and research that made this book possible. I would also like to extend my appreciation to Jack A. Meyer for his helpful suggestions and to Melinda Kicherer for her administrative assistance.

M.E.L.

Library of Congress Cataloging in Publication Data

Main entry under title:

The Health policy agenda.

    (Studies in health policy)
    1. Medical policy—United States—Addresses, essays,
lectures.   2. Medical economics—United States—
Addresses, essays, lectures.   3. Medical care—United
States—Addresses, essays, lectures.   I. Lewin, Marion
Ein.   II. American Enterprise Institute for Public
Policy Research.   III. Series. [DNLM: 1. Delivery of
Health Care—economics—United States.   2. Economics,
Medical—trends—United States.   3. Financing, Govern-
ment—economics—United States.   4. Health Policy—
economics—United States.   W 74HH4364]
RA395.A3.H4255   1985   338.4'73621'0973   85-20159

ISBN 0-8447-3584-1
ISBN 0-8447-3583-3 (pbk)
AEI Studies 427
1 3 5 7 9 10 8 6 4 2

Printed in the United States of America

Contents

Foreword

The seven papers in this volume, commissioned under a grant to AEI from the Pew Memorial Trust, address some of the major health policy issues shaping today's rapidly changing health care environment. Approximately three years ago, the Pew Memorial Trust launched a major initiative, the Pew Health Policy Program, to provide current and potential leaders in health care decision making specialized postgraduate training and an opportunity to expand their knowledge of relevant policy concerns and the policy process. Several leading institutions across the country were chosen to develop special programs in health: Boston University/Brandeis University, the University of California at San Francisco, the University of Michigan, and the Rand Corporation/University of California, Los Angeles.

A fifth grant was awarded to AEI's Center for Health Policy Research to conduct two major conferences each year for fellows and faculty participating in the program. Not only do these seminars provide a forum in which fellows and faculty can share their professional experiences and research activities, but they also give participants a chance to engage in dialogue with key national, state, and local health policy makers from both the public and private sectors.

The commissioned papers that appear in this book—essays written by acknowledged experts in their respective fields—have greatly enriched seminar activities. Evaluative and pragmatic, they serve not only as background papers for discussion among those scholars who participate in the health policy program but as forward-looking syntheses of major health public policy concerns designed to appeal to a broad audience.

The papers cover timely topics that are relevant to the current debate over the future of health care financing and delivery in a world of limited resources. The changes in physician/hospital relations; the future of technology under a new government payment system; the growing problem of our nation's uninsured and underinsured; the challenge of a graying America, with the urgency to develop more rational policies regarding long-term care; the impact on states and regions of new government policies including cuts in grants-in-aid; and the ethical implications of a more restricted, market-oriented health care system are all highlighted.

AEI's Center for Health Policy Research is particularly pleased to be involved in the Pew Health Policy Program because of our own long involvement in studying new directions in health policy and disseminating the results of our research, site visits, and convening activities throughout the public and private sectors.

The Health Policy Agenda: Some Critical Questions is the second in what we expect will be a series of publications based on scholarly papers commissioned for the Pew Health Policy Program. *Incentives vs. Controls in Health Policy: Broadening the Debate,* edited by Jack A. Meyer, director of AEI's Center for Health Policy Research, was published earlier this year.

WILLIAM J. BAROODY, JR.
President
American Enterprise Institute

Contributors

ALEXANDER MORGAN CAPRON holds the new Norman Topping Chair in Law, Medicine, and Public Policy at the University of Southern California. From 1980 to 1983 he served as executive director of the President's Commission for the Study of Ethical Problems in Medicine and Biomedical and Behavioral Research. Mr. Capron is a member of the Institute of Society, Ethics, and Life Sciences, Hastings-on-Hudson, New York, and the National Academy of Science's Institute of Medicine.

MICHAEL CHAPKO is a research associate professor in the Department of Community Dentistry and Health Services at the University of Washington. He has a doctorate in social psychology from Hunter College of the City University of New York.

DOUGLAS CONRAD is an associate professor and director of the graduate program in health services administration, Department of Health Services, at the University of Washington. He has a doctorate in economics and finance from the University of Chicago Graduate School of Business. Dr. Conrad is an advanced fellow in health services administration at the American Hospital Association/Blue Cross Association. He is on the Board of Editors for the *Journal of Health Politics, Policy, and Law* and the Health Administration Press.

KAREN COOK is a professor in the Department of Sociology at the University of Washington. She has a doctorate in sociology from Stanford University.

RUTH S. HANFT is an independent consultant in health policy research. Mrs. Hanft served as deputy assistant secretary for health policy and deputy assistant secretary for health research during the Carter administration. She recently completed studies for the Michigan State Legislature on the costs of medical education for minorities in the health professions and on strategic plans for teaching hospitals and academic health centers. In addition, she has written extensively on health manpower, academic health centers, hospital cost containment, and technology assessment.

MARION EIN LEWIN is the associate director of AEI's Center for Health Policy Research. From 1978 to 1983 she served as associate director of the National Health Policy Forum, a nonpartisan educational program for high-level federal, state, and private-sector specialists in health affairs. She has written on a wide range of subjects in the health care area including special articles and studies on indigent care. At present Ms. Lewin directs the semiannual Pew Health Policy Program conferences.

VICTOR J. MILLER is creator and director of Federal Funds Information for States, a joint project of the National Governors' Association and the National Conference of State Legislatures, that tracks the distribution of federal government funds among the states. Mr. Miller has also served as a senior analyst for the Senate Budget Committee, and from 1972 to 1979 he worked at the Office of Management and Budget as the primary staff expert on grants-in-aid to state and local governments.

MICHAEL MORRISEY is a senior economist at the American Hospital Association and associate director of the AHA's Hospital Research and Educational Trust. He has a doctorate in economics from the University of Wisconsin.

STEPHEN SHORTELL is A. C. Buehler Distinguished Professor of hospital health services management and professor of organization behavior at Northwestern University. He has a doctorate in business from the University of Chicago.

BRUCE C. VLADECK is president of the United Hospital Fund of New York. Before joining the fund in 1983, Dr. Vladeck was assistant vice-president of the Robert Wood Johnson Foundation. From 1979 to 1982, he was director of the New Jersey Health Planning and Development Agency and oversaw the development and implementation of that state's all-payer, DRG-based hospital prospective payment system. Dr. Vladeck is the author of *Unloving Care: The Nursing Home Tragedy*.

JUDITH L. WAGNER is a senior analyst at the U.S. Congressional Office of Technology Assessment (OTA), specializing in health programs.

She has written extensively in the areas of technology assessment and payment policies. Before coming to OTA, Dr. Wagner was a senior research associate at the Urban Institute. She was recently elected to serve on the board of the Association of Health Services Research (AHSR). Dr. Wagner has her doctorate from Cornell University.

Introduction

Marion Ein Lewin

Sweeping and profound changes are taking place in this country's financing and delivery patterns for medical care. Leaving behind the days when a health care payment system was often described as an open-ended, blank-check arrangement, Americans have entered an era when prudent purchasing has become the rallying cry for both public and private payers of care. From a widely held perception that more is always better in the realm of health care services, we have now arrived at a keen awareness that we live in a world of limited resources, a place where trade-offs must be made.

Whereas in the recent past the federal government sought to play a leading role in designing the shape and direction of the nation's health care system, today it wants to limit its fiscal exposure and, to that end, has granted the states and the private sector significantly more flexibility and power to reform health care and contain costs. Although many people have greeted the greater influence of market forces as a welcome trend, society in general continues to believe that health care is a special commodity, one that should be treated differently from other goods and services in our economy.

These often contradictory dynamics have ushered in a time of considerable flux and uncertainty. In an environment of constraints, how will resources be allocated among the rich and poor, among providers and consumers of care? What should be the role and responsibility of government in a more market-oriented environment? The essays in this volume attempt to shed light on some of these compelling questions by looking at premises that have guided health policy in the past and by examining several alternative approaches that have been put forward as more appropriate for today's realities.

The first two chapters in the book address what has become an issue of primary concern. Health care, some have observed, is becoming a membership affair; those without the financial wherewithal to pay for medical services may increasingly be denied access. Estimates

1

indicate that 25 million to 35 million Americans lack health care coverage. Studies show that persons without insurance, even when they are ill, use health care services less frequently than those with insurance. The sick who are uninsured and poor make only half as many physician visits as those on Medicaid and incur 50 percent fewer hospital stays. At the same time, costly new technologies continue to be developed, bringing the likely prospect that ability to pay will become a key criterion of how such medical advances are allocated.

Alexander Capron's chapter outlines how a workable ethical framework might be applied to health policy decision making and how it could help us deal more effectively with issues of access and equity in a period of finite resources. Capron argues that pursuing public policies that seek to guarantee an individual's "right" to health care are simply unrealistic. To adopt such approaches creates obligations that are impossible to meet and, as a result, fails to resolve fundamental issues as they relate to the distribution of health care resources.

Emphasizing the need to frame ethical principles that offer humane and morally defensible allocation guidelines, Capron builds on the valuable work he did with the President's Commission for the Study of Ethical Problems in Medicine and Biomedical and Behavioral Research, by arguing for a strategy that would ensure "equitable access" to health care for all Americans, which means access to an "adequate" level of care without incurring "excessive burden" in obtaining such care.

Formulating a workable definition of adequacy and excessive burden must necessarily go beyond a calculation of precisely measurable factors. The definition must include judgments about fairness that Capron contends can best be achieved through a process in which key participants attempt to develop and employ a common language for judging the ethical aspects of existing medical care practices, as well as of those treatments and technologies newly proposed.

Marion Ein Lewin's overview of the indigent care issue drives home to us why the problem of the uninsured and underinsured has become such a critical public policy concern and underscores the patchwork quilt character of many of the current programs intended to serve this population. Approximately half of the nation's poor are not currently covered by Medicaid, for example. Since states have wide discretion in determining eligibility, scope of benefits, and payment standards under this major health care program for the poor, entitlement is often more a function of where a person or family resides than of documented need.

Both the public and private sectors are now trying to enhance coverage for the underinsured with the objectives of spending limited dollars more cost effectively and distributing the burden more equitably among purchasers of care. Policy makers are becoming increasingly aware that the development of a more competitive health care marketplace may falter if it disregards those without the means to finance their care and that we must concentrate our efforts on providing a realistic but fair and adequate level of care for all Americans.

Victor Miller's chapter, "Recent Changes in Federal Grants and State Budgets," highlights a topic with which many students of health public policy have only fleeting familiarity but which is of great importance given the larger role states have been asked to play in the provision of social welfare services. According to Miller, federal grants-in-aid reached their peak in 1978 but have since steadily declined as a share of the federal budget. Miller describes some of the key events—overall cutbacks and restructuring; the introduction of 1980 census data into grants-in-aid distributional formulas; variations among the states in economic performance—that have produced significant shifts in the number and amounts of grants and their distribution among the states. Much grants-in-aid spending is tied to economic conditions and designed to be countercyclical. Despite this intent, Miller points out, the interstate impact is often just the reverse, because of the time lag in data. For example, of the fourteen states that lost employment between 1979 and 1981, six also suffered decreases in their fiscal year 1982/1983 Medicaid match, because the match was based on data from 1977–1979, before employment began to decline. Similarly, the four largest increases in Medicaid matching funds for fiscal year 1982/1983 went to states with increasing employment. Regardless of states' needs, we find in looking at the future that federal matching rates for fiscal year 1986/1987 have already been established, based on 1981–1983 data.

As a result of economic recovery and fiscal austerity—and the fact that all states except Vermont have constitutional or statutory requirements for balanced budgets—many states are faring better today than in 1982 and 1983. There appears to be an ongoing struggle, however, especially in states with large urban areas, to provide an adequate safety net for the poor and the homeless. The administration's most recent proposal to cap Medicaid program costs has not been accepted by Congress, in light of the major funding cuts in entitlement programs for the poor enacted as part of the Omnibus

Reconciliation Act of 1981 (OBRA). Nevertheless, the president's fiscal year 1986 budget has indicated cuts amounting to $8 billion for state-operating and capital grants-in-aid programs. There are, moreover, strong possibilities that the administration may use the relatively better fiscal health of the states to redirect tax revenues from state to federal coffers in order to cut the federal deficit.

Diminished funding at a time of growing need has been a primary factor in the enthusiastic support in several states for hospital rate-setting programs. In recent years ten states have adopted some form of this strategy to reduce the rate of increase of hospital costs and to distribute more equitably the burden of indigent care. Douglas Conrad and his colleagues give us an insightful analysis of the economic incentives created by the structural characteristics of these programs, called all-payer rate-setting systems, stressing those elements that, in their view, are the most pertinent for predicting the degree of effect on hospitals.

Today hospital rate setting seems to be moving into a new generation. New York has decided, and other states may yet decide, not to renew the Medicare all-payer waiver but to rely instead on a prospective pricing system based on diagnosis-related groups (DRGs). Some states are opting for a blend of market and regulatory approaches to bring about savings and systems reform. As we try different types of reimbursement controls, the Conrad paper is particularly relevant in its assessment of the behavioral responses of providers to varied economic incentives.

Judith Wagner's chapter, "DRGs and Other Payment Groupings: The Impact on Medical Practice and Technology," takes on an issue of special concern to health policy makers. Although few people disagree that the new Medicare prospective payment system has made hospitals more cost conscious and has intensified competition among health care providers, its long-term prognosis as an effective and viable payment model remains open to debate. A key question, frequently raised, is what effect DRGs will have on the research, development, and diffusion of new technologies. Although observers have predicted that per case payment creates incentives for hospitals to adopt new cost-saving technologies and to restrain themselves from purchasing equipment that is likely to increase the cost of patient care, Wagner says that technologies are neither cost saving nor cost raising independent of the context in which they are used. Thus hospitals cannot be expected to behave similarly as a result of the new Medicare pricing structure; rather they will target their responses more specifically to the geographical and competitive environment in which they operate. Wagner contends that the ultimate success or failure of the DRG payment model will rest on the system's ability to adopt and encourage appropriate technological changes in medicine, including the development of technologies that may be cost raising but are needed and beneficial. The paper suggests some ways these objectives might be accomplished.

The turbulent forces currently at work in the health care system demonstrate that the fundamental assumptions about health care practices are changing on many levels. Ruth Hanft, from her extensive experience as a health policy specialist, offers a timely and insightful picture of how hospitals are learning to operate in a dramatically different climate. New payment systems, funding cutbacks, and growing cost consciousness on the part of purchasers are forcing hospitals to redefine their mission and to reassess the types of patients they seek to attract and the services they want to provide. Marketing and diversification have become survival tools in a world of competition and limited dollars. Hanft's article focuses attention on another major trend operating in today's health care scene: in a few years we have moved from a shortage to an oversupply of physicians. This phenomenon, in and of itself, has already unleashed major changes in the way medicine will be practiced in the future.

Although a high level of experimentation and creativity characterizes many aspects of health care financing and delivery today, Bruce Vladeck, in the last chapter, addresses one dimension—long-term care—in which new approaches appear to be in short supply. Americans sixty-five-years old and older compose the fastest-growing segment of the nation's population. The latest projections of the U.S. Census Bureau estimate that, by the year 2050, 21.7 percent of the population is likely to be over sixty-five, up from the present 11.4 percent. The percentage that will be eighty-five or older will grow from 1 percent to 5.2 percent.

While the graying of America portends a substantial increase in demand for services, current public programs for the elderly, such as Medicare and Medicaid, are poorly targeted. They provide extensive coverage for certain acute care services but little or no protection for other services needed in the later years of life.

Few will argue with Vladeck's assertion that we must abandon our policy of stasis in this vital area and investigate avenues that may improve the organization and integration of long-term care services, as well as more appropriately mesh public and private dollars. Vladeck contends, however, that up to now policy makers have shown no serious commitment to move in such a direction.

As this book is being readied for publication in midsummer 1985,

5

the far-reaching restructuring and diversification taking place in health care are receiving front-page attention. Public and private payers, intent on making the system more affordable and efficient, are using their purchasing power to reshape the financing and delivery of health care services. Consumers, better informed and increasingly armed with choices and more of a financial stake, are choosing facilities that hold promise of using limited dollars more effectively and appropriately. The newly vitalized medical marketplace, however, has brought to the fore several major public policy concerns. As providers of care are forced to operate in a more competitive, price-oriented environment, the country is witnessing the gradual disenfranchisement of those Americans without the ability to pay for their health care. With medical knowledge continuing to expand and technological advancement continuing to unfold, we find ourselves headed toward a future in which scarce resources will be allocated on ability to pay, rather than on the basis of equity or need. Because changing demographics foretoken a growing elderly population, we recognize that we must formulate more coherent and viable long-term care strategies for the aged, the chronically ill, and the disabled.

Clearly, the challenge today is to confront current economic realities without losing sight of the compassion and the commitment to excellence and quality that have for so long characterized our nation's system of health care delivery. While there are no easy answers as to how to accomplish this goal, these essays offer some valuable food for thought about how to proceed.

1

Allocating Finite Resources: Questions of Equity and Access

Alexander Morgan Capron

Introduction: Any Role for Ethics?

I am often asked to comment on the contribution that ethical analysis might make to the health public policy debate, a dialogue in which many questions are currently being raised about the ends to which the health care system is—and ought to be —devoted and about the means used to reach those ends. The reasons cited for what is unquestionably a major reexamination of the field are many:

• the rapid and seemingly inexorable rise in health care expenditures—in annual percentage terms, in absolute terms, and as a percentage of GNP and of government expenditures at all levels;
• the increasing role of for-profit institutions and multi-institution systems in providing health care (with resulting changes in the management style of nonprofit institutions);
• dramatic biomedical developments, such as the artificial heart, which highlight the increasing role that new (and usually expensive) technology plays in health care, especially for acutely ill patients.

I believe that ethical analysis can make several contributions to the process of reexamining health policy. First, there are at least as many "solutions" suggested as there are issues. Indeed, each year professional journals are filled with suggestions, federal departments make proposals, congressional committees study new laws, and state and local officials try out regulatory schemes, from the innovative to the shopworn. Even when new programs are adopted, they are soon up for alteration or, perhaps, a thorough overhaul at the hands of both administrators and legislators. Health policy needs a clear— and clearly defensible—ethical basis if it is going to succeed, to survive the pressures of the moment, and to be fair.

I believe that articulating such an ethical framework is possible, and, indeed, that a useful and sound beginning of such an articulation has already been made. Health planners, economists, and others concerned with the medical, economic, and organizational sides of health policy making will find devoting some of their efforts toward this end worthwhile. Similarly, as one who believes that ethical analysis is greatly enhanced by a firm grounding in reality, I believe that the process of trying to elaborate society's basic ethical framework for providing health care requires the assistance of people experienced in all aspects of health policy.

Donald V. Seibert, the retired chairman of J. C. Penney, in defending against claims of eroding ethical standards in U.S. business, recently argued that "the more energy corporate America devotes to examining its ethical standards, the freer executives will be to make the tough decisions that reflect the larger view and the stronger they will be to resist questionable actions for a quick fix."[1] In my view, the same argument is substantially true for health policy.

Ethical analysis can also elucidate the effects on the health care system of the norms and practices that govern the physician-patient relationship. For many years, the attention of most people who examined medical ethics was on the physician-patient relationship and was carried out largely in terms of traditional philosophical categories (utilitarian, deontological, and so forth). About fifteen years ago, both the categories and the questions began to broaden, stimulated in particular by biomedical developments (such as psychosurgery, heart transplantation, and genetic engineering) that seemed to challenge many traditional notions, not merely of health care but of health itself. As bioethics developed, it became apparent that the questions being raised could not be adequately examined solely within the confines of the physician-patient relationship but had to draw on theories (about community, justice, beneficence) that took account of others besides the physician and patient who must play significant parts in any resolution of the questions.

Some conclusions have emerged from more than a decade of this bioethical analysis, although the results are not clear. In effect, the second contribution of ethics for our present purposes is to shine a light on some of the ethical difficulties that arise in medical care and, consequently, to emphasize their importance for anyone trying to address the issue of allocating finite resources.

Ethical Obligations as a Bedrock of Policy

My first assertion has two components: first, that an ethical framework is essential for defensible health policy; and, second, that a specific ethical framework is correct. Although I put the assertion forward in the form of a thesis that I will try to demonstrate, many questions can be raised along the way. I hope that my argument will serve as a stimulus for readers to pursue these questions, even if their answers would cast doubt on the thesis itself.

To explore my thesis, I must establish several propositions: first, that there is a problem of access to health care in the United States; second, that this problem demands a special ethical response because of the special nature of health care; third, that this response is best framed in terms of an ethical obligation on the part of society rather than in terms of a right on the part of individuals, despite the usual correlation of one person's obligation with another person's right; and, fourth, that the societal obligation is to ensure that everyone has access to an adequate level of health care without imposing excessive burdens on anyone in obtaining that care.

Is Access a Problem? When the President's Commission for the Study of Ethical Problems in Medicine and Biomedical and Behavioral Research began its work in 1980, one of its mandated subjects was a study of the ethical implications of "differences in the availability of health services" among various groups in the United States.[2] The members of the President's Commission were physicians, researchers, and informed members of related professions. Thus it may seem surprising to readers who are well versed in the health policy literature that the general view of the President's Commission at the beginning was that, while there might turn out to be a few remaining differences in the availability of care for particular groups in the country (especially those living in isolated locales), no real problem of "access to health care exists today. For most Americans, the adoption of Medicare and Medicaid in the mid-1960s was believed to have solved the access problem." Not surprisingly, three years later as the commission wound up its work on this and other projects, the commissioners had come to a different understanding of the extent of the access problem.

As we well know, the data are complex and often difficult to interpret. In examining any particular issue several variables may be used. For example, in measuring health care one can look to the physical availability of health services to a consumer or group of consumers; or, more broadly, one can examine whether or not there are barriers to people's ability to obtain available services. Some obstacles are likely to be difficult to measure, such as the impediment that a complex health care system imposes on those who have difficulties in negotiating their way through such a system. Others are

9

more straightforward, such as the barrier imposed by an absence of insurance.

Insurance protection against the high cost of medical care can no longer be viewed as optional; it has become essential. More is at stake than the risk of financial ruin, which is the usual concern of insurance. Today people without some health insurance face delays in obtaining care and in some cases experience the outright refusal of care by providers. Moreover, anticipating that they may face costs they cannot afford or may be rebuffed by physicians and hospitals if they lack the guarantee of an insurance plan, the uninsured are slower to seek care.

Of course, this problem is not major for most Americans, since about 70 percent of the population is insured through some form of privately funded insurance, typically obtained at the workplace. Furthermore, people associated with the military have long been provided health care at government expense, and Medicare and Medicaid have extended public financing to millions of elderly and poor Americans who formerly had either no insurance protection or inadequate coverage. Consequently, about an additional 20 percent of the population now obtains primary protection under some form of publicly financed health coverage. Nonetheless, the President's Commission—consistent with others who have studied the subject—found that 8.6 percent of the population has no insurance during the course of an entire year and another 7.5 percent is uninsured during part of the year, meaning that between 22 million and 25 million people lack insurance coverage at any one time.[3] During a period of high unemployment these figures will increase; indeed, early in 1983 the Congressional Budget Office indicated that the number of people lacking health coverage had been swollen by an additional 10 million workers and their family members who were without insurance coverage as a result of the economic recession of 1981–1982.

Lack of insurance is most pronounced among the very poor, the near-poor, racial and ethnic minorities, and the residents of rural areas. Many people less than sixty-five-years old whose income places them below the federally established poverty level are, nevertheless, ineligible for their state's Medicaid program; yet they are much too poor to purchase private health insurance. Indeed, approximately half of the poor are not covered by Title XIX. When the poor do obtain care, they not only spend a much larger proportion of their income for out-of-pocket health care expenses—10.2 percent for those with incomes below $3,000 versus 1.7 percent for those with incomes above $15,000 (as of 1977)—but also actually spend a larger dollar amount.

10

The current pattern of insurance coverage resembles a patchwork quilt, with coverage depending in large part on where a person lives, whether and where a person is employed, and whether the person meets specific requirements to qualify for coverage under a categorical public program.

The lack of access to care can have serious health, economic, and social consequences for society as a whole as well as for affected individuals. The most obvious of these consequences is that people affected by the lack of access may go without needed services and suffer the consequences. Financial barriers to health care, especially among the poor, have been shown to affect health status. The data show that the poor are significantly less healthy than the nonpoor by any established measure, and yet they receive less adequate medical attention. In the commission's view, the inability to pay appeared to be a critical factor affecting entry into the health care system and an important determinant of the use of services.

People with limited access to care may delay in acquiring care or may defer needed treatment. Evidence suggests that such people are more likely to be hospitalized after their illnesses have reached an advanced stage. Delays in care can have significant health consequences, and many conditions that are amenable to timely medical treatment can, if neglected, develop serious complications. Patients entering the hospital with conditions in advanced stages use more diagnostic tests and ancillary services than people who are hospitalized at earlier stages of their illnesses. Thus lack of access to adequate care at an appropriate time is not only inequitable but can also generate greater total costs for the health care system.

Why Is Health Care Special? That some people lack access to health care would not be a problem if health care were not an item of considerable value. Indeed, at an earlier time in history—not too long ago—when physicians could do much less than was beneficial for patients and often caused more harm than they avoided—brushing off concerns about lack of access to care might have been possible. Today, however, the availability of health services of all sorts, preventative as well as acute, nursing as well as medical, has a demonstrable effect in reducing morbidity and mortality rates. One clear proof of this statement comes from comparing our age-adjusted death rates with those of other countries in the Western world. From 1955 to 1967 we lagged behind most other countries in this regard; after Medicare was enacted, we led most other countries, with a marked improvement in death rates among the elderly.

Health care's special value derives from its importance in relieving suffering, in preventing premature death, and in restoring normal

11

functioning. These are all what philosophers call "primary goods," since one does not need to know a particular person's aims or preferences to know that health is good for that person. Health care is also valued for its role in increasing opportunity (by restoring a person to normal functioning), in providing information about an individual's condition, and in giving evidence of our mutual empathy, compassion, and solidarity in the face of suffering, illness, and death.

A further aspect of this issue gets into more controversial ground, where people with empirical knowledge could make a contribution. To assert that health care is special is for some to suggest that it ought not to be governed entirely by the usual rules of the marketplace. Typically, when people want something in our society, they have to pay for it. Their willingness to pay is a measure of their desire to obtain it; their ability to pay is determined by the value placed on the services they (or someone who has made them a beneficiary) provide to society for which they receive an economic reward. With other necessities of life—such as food and housing— the problems that arise with the use of a market are significant only for those people who have too few resources to obtain even a subsistence level. For the rest, variations in the luxury of one's accommodations or the richness of one's diet are morally acceptable if not desirable in a democratic and egalitarian society. One might say that it is expected that with a little thought and discipline a person can divide up his or her budget in a way that ensures enough funds for the necessities, since these needs can be fairly well anticipated.

The same is not true of health care, however. Not only is the distribution of ill health very uneven within a population and for any individual over a lifetime, but some illnesses and injuries can lead to medical and hospital bills that would be catastrophic for any but the most wealthy members of society. The empirical question that lurks here is simply the extent to which ill health is unevenly distributed, so that an individual could not necessarily be expected to anticipate it and make adequate financial preparation.

Another factor that makes health care special is the undeserved nature of most differences in the need for such care. This is obviously a controversial matter and one on which evidence is still being developed. There are certainly some forms of behavior (for example, smoking) that are statistically linked with higher incidence of certain diseases. Before concluding that this finding disputes what we regard as the special nature of health care, however, a policy analyst would have to be convinced (1) that a particular lifestyle or behavior has a measurable adverse effect on health status, (2) that the individual has the power to alter that lifestyle or behavior voluntarily to improve health, and (3) that it is fair to single out a particular lifestyle or behavior while doing nothing about others the influence of which, though as great or greater, is as yet unproven. Furthermore, beyond identifying something as a morally significant and voluntary choice, one would have to be convinced that there is an adequate means of informing people, in a way that makes sense to them, about a particular behavior and its connection with a health risk. Again, these are matters on which more empirical information would certainly be desirable. For the moment, it seems fair to say that differences in the need for health services ought not to be given much, if any, moral weight in deciding who gets treated.

Individual Right or Societal Obligation? If the need for health services is distributed largely in a manner not based on moral deserving and if many individuals have insufficient resources to pay for such services, how ought a just society respond? If we had asked that question a generation ago, the answer would probably have been that society should guarantee the right of each person to obtain health care. Indeed, the President's Commission on the Health Needs of the Nation concluded in 1952 that "access to the means for the attainment and preservation of health is a basic human right."[4] Although this formulation is appealing—and, as a political matter, doubtless contributed to the emergence of the consensus that led to the adoption of our major health care financing programs of the 1960s—it has distinct drawbacks.

First, when one moves from a rhetorical level to an examination of the law, such a right disappears. Neither the U.S. Supreme Court nor any federal appellate court has found a constitutional right to government-funded health care, much less a right to health. Of course, once a health care program or financing scheme is established by the legislature, everyone who is eligible may have a constitutionally protected right to be fairly considered for inclusion. It is remarkable, however, how much leeway the courts have given officials in administering such plans in ways that narrow the benefits provided and the classes of potential recipients.[5]

Second, to speak of a "right" fails to address the harder question: "a right to *what*?" As much as one might wish, there is no way to ensure each person a right to health. Despite everyone's best efforts, some people become sick and disabled and die prematurely; the proclamation of a right of health cannot alter this fact. Phrasing the right as one to health care rather than to health helps somewhat, but leaves the question, How much health care? In a society that

13

proclaims equality as a basic value, the answer may be "to an equal amount of health care." Yet this formulation is also impractical and even rather silly. Some fortunate people go through life seldom needing medical attention; others are chronically ill. To provide everyone with an equal amount of care would thus be both wasteful and unfair.

Equal treatment is thus a very poor answer to the question "access to what?" Of course, this question has to be answered under any formulation even if such an answer is tentative and imperfect. The point here is simply that—because of certain tendencies in our legal and political systems—a rights-based formulation is more likely to be framed in terms of equality than are other ethical responses to the uneven distribution of health status and resources.

The third drawback to framing society's response in terms of a right to health care is that the expansive nature of such a right (for the reasons just surveyed) may actually undermine efforts to remedy the problems of access to care. A more reasonable statement of the amount of care or financial support owed is needed if the assertion is going to be met with a positive response, especially in the present climate of heavy emphasis on cost-containment and of worries about the long-term viability of the Medicare program.

If one were to recognize a right to health care, one would expect to be able to state a reciprocal obligation on the part of society to ensure the fulfillment of this right.[6] The converse is not necessarily the case, however. There are times when one person or a group of persons has an obligation without creating a complementary right for anyone else, at least not an enforceable one. For example, society may have a moral obligation to help the needy and would be subject to serious moral criticism for failing to do so; yet the needy would not be able to demand such aid as their due without legislation that made it so.

Just as the existence of an obligation does not always imply a corresponding right, so collective obligations exist even when individuals have no enforceable right. For example, the government is supposed to maintain civil order and provide adequate defenses against attack, but its failure to do so does not breach the rights of individuals within the society. Consequently, in the area of health care, it is not only sensible but philosophically sound to provide an analysis based on a societal obligation even if one declines to construct one based on enforceable individual rights. (This formulation depends on some feelings of community and identity within the society, which provide the predicate for a sense of duty; it does not, however, necessarily lodge this obligation with the government.)

What Is the Nature of the Obligation? The objective of this analysis is to define the response of a just society faced with problems of access to health care. Thus the societal obligation can logically be expressed as an ethical obligation to ensure *equitable access* to health care for all. What, then, is the meaning of equity in this context?

One possible meaning of equity—that of equality—was considered previously as part of the discussion of a right to health. "In this view, it follows that if a given level of care is available to one individual it must be available to all."[7] The problems with this approach are manifest: a standard of care set high, compared with that now being received, could lead to disproportionate resources being devoted to health care; if, to avoid this draining effect, the standard of care were set low, services would have to be denied to some people who want them and would now purchase them in preference to other uses of their own funds. Perverse effects can be expected from a standard of equality, not merely because of differences in people's wealth and income but, more basically, because of differences in preferences—comparing health with other values and goals and comparing various aspects of health with the nonfinancial sacrifices one must make to achieve them.

Another alternative would be to say that society has an obligation to ensure access to care that may be beneficial. Although this formulation recognizes the individual variations that a standard of equality overlooks, it too has unacceptable implications. "Unless health is the only good or resources are unlimited, it would be irrational for a society—as for an individual—to make a commitment to provide whatever health care might be beneficial regardless of cost."[8] There are a great many other uses for the resources that could go into health care, and any society will need to take those other uses—the "opportunity costs" of providing particular treatments—into account when defining its obligation to ensure equitable access to health care. Consequently, some health services can ethically be left out of the societal obligation, not because they provide no benefit but because they provide too few benefits in relation to their costs, compared with other uses of the same resources.

Some people have suggested that defining access according to need rather than benefit would provide a more sensible benchmark for equitable treatment. Assuming that one can avoid the problem of equating need with benefit (that is, if medical need is defined as a condition for which medical care might be effective), the term "need" might actually prove more expansive. If need were self-defined, it would be nothing more than a personal desire or preference. Conversely, if need were narrowly defined, it might encompass

15

only a minimal level of services, such as that level needed to prevent death.

These other definitions having failed, a better definition of equitable access might emerge if we referred back to those factors that make health care a matter of special importance in the first place. The societal obligation can thus be seen as ensuring a level of health care adequate "to achieve sufficient welfare, opportunity, information, and evidence of interpersonal concern, to facilitate a reasonably full and satisfying life."[9] To formulate the standard as "an adequate level" recognizes that society need not secure for everyone all the care he or she may want and that priorities have to be set in light of there being other goods besides health. Moreover, the standard is manifestly dependent on time and place; residents of a prosperous country with many technological resources will have a different view of the full and satisfying life than those in a poorer country and, hence, a different view about what level of care is adequate to fulfill society's obligation. Finally, such a standard does not insist that anyone's liberty be restricted to keep him or her from obtaining care above the adequate level, as would a standard based on equality of health care.

In addition to ensuring that everyone can obtain an adequate level of care, an equitable system will also avoid imposing excessive burdens on anyone, in terms of financial costs, waiting and travel time, and ancillary factors (such as costs of transportation). Such burdens might otherwise deter some people from receiving needed care; for others, the burdens would be borne but only at the expense of their ability to meet other needs in their lives. Certainly it would be both illogical and unfair to establish a system intended to ensure health care because of its contribution to welfare and opportunity if the system required many people to forgo other things (such as food, shelter, or education) that are also needed for basic welfare and opportunity. This is not to say that burdens must be identical for all but merely that they must fall within an acceptable range. Marked differences would be cause for careful scrutiny, though they would not, per se, be unacceptable.

Plainly, for this definition of equitable access (an adequate level of care without excessive burdens in obtaining it) to be helpful, we must further define "adequacy" and "excessiveness." This task should not be thought of as abstract or academic. Rather, the concepts will be shaped and refined as they are actually used to compare new and existing health policies. Even as the concepts are clarified, however, I would not expect them to become simple measuring rods; reasonable people may still find room to disagree. What is crucial is (1) that people agree on the goal of ensuring equitable access to health care for all Americans and (2) that the relative advantages and disadvantages of alternative policies are judged on ethical as well as on economic and scientific grounds, by comparing the extent to which the policies ensure an adequate level of care for all members of society without imposing excessive burdens in the process. A commitment to seek equity in health care is thus, in part, a commitment to a process which the participants attempt to develop and employ a common framework for judging the ethical aspects of each new proposal and of existing systems.

Certain parts of that common framework can be sketched already. For one thing, the notion of adequacy must be multifaceted. One component will be the judgment of health professionals (notably, though not exclusively, physicians) about the medical necessity of any particular service. That component cannot be the sole determinant of adequacy, however, for several reasons. First, health professionals "have no special expertise in deciding how the effects of medical care ought to be valued, either with respect to the relative value of different dimensions of care or, particularly, the value attached to health care relative to other goods."[10] The struggle that women have had in the past twenty years to force the health care system to provide alternative forms of prenatal and obstetrical care is merely one illustration of the possible divergence of professionals' views from those of the population as a whole.

Second, and more important, sole reliance on professional judgment would almost certainly inflate the notion of adequacy, because health professionals have traditionally tended to provide all care that is even possibly beneficial (especially when their own income is tied in some way to the amount of care provided). Thus professsional judgment provides a good criterion for exclusion (that is, a particular service would not be part of the adequate level of care if found wanting on scientific or medical grounds), but professional judgment alone is not a conclusive criterion for inclusion.

Another measure of adequacy could start with the level of care now obtained by the average person, on the premise that, with a generally satisfactory health care system, current usage is a realistic measure of what people regard as adequate. Again, however, this measure cannot be used without some modifications to compensate for certain distortions in the present system. For example, health care is not currently purchased in a marketplace by informed consumers but is prescribed by health professionals. Current utilization patterns, then, may be merely a proxy for professionals' judgment (which has already been taken into account). The mix of services may say more

17

about health professionals' biases than about what the general public would really regard as adequate.

Health insurance insulates many individuals from the financial consequences of their use of health care services—particularly people provided generous employment-related benefit packages. Therefore a more accurate measure of adequate health care would be the level of care that people of average means would purchase for themselves and their families, or, if that is regarded as too unrealistic (since prudent people would insure against medical misfortunes, rather than attempting to pay out-of-pocket as they arise), the level of care for which people of average means would be willing to spend their income, assuming that such income were treated no differently (for employment or tax purposes) than that used to purchase other necessities. Health planners can identify sources of such data or can suggest how information of this sort could be constructed by reanalyzing existing insurance data.

Relying solely on a list of services, such as that included in the 1973 Health Maintenance Organization (HMO) Act, would be inappropriate because individuals obtain such different benefits from the same services that what would be inadequate in one case might be excessive in another. Such a list, however, can be used to help evaluate the adequacy of particular health policies and plans. If a list of services were combined with factors such as professional judgment, the result would be comparable to the review process used by most health insurance programs to determine the appropriateness and efficiency of a service before reimbursing for it.

In the end, the combination of these and other measures of adequacy should lead to a process that is itself comparative, beginning with those services that would be widely regarded as part of any definition of adequate health care (for example, prenatal care and treatment of common acute infections). From this core of agreement, one would attempt to move outward, by weighing the burden to the patient and the cost of each treatment against the effectiveness of the treatment in preserving life, easing pain, and restoring functioning, as compared with other conditions and treatments about which consensus already existed.

The comparative aspect of the process of determining an adequate level of care would be especially useful when proposals were made not for a wholly new structure (that is, a change in the tax system or in Medicare deductibles) but for the inclusion of particular treatments within the existing financing framework. We have recently seen this happen in the case of liver transplantation, for example.[11] An equitable system would require a means—such as that which the National Center for Health Care Technology was beginning to provide before it was unceremoniously eliminated[12]—for comparing new treatments with those already included, on such grounds as comparability of the risk or of the disability that the treatment remedies, the degree of success achieved, and the burden and cost entailed. The fact that the decision is ultimately a *judgment* about fairness and not merely a *calculation* of precisely measurable factors emphasizes the need for an open and creative process, without undue deference to expertise. Moreover, the focus of such a process ought not to be solely on a few, new high-technology items; everything we know about health care costs suggests that the "little ticket" items deserve just as close a look as the big tickets.[13]

Basically, a similar process would be followed for defining "excessive burdens," drawing on professional and lay views and comparative measures. Again, it should be possible to begin with a core of agreement—for example, that a financial burden is too great when it precludes a family from purchasing other necessities such as food and shelter.

Applying the Goal of Equitable Access. Without exaggerating the importance of the type of analysis offered by the President's Commission on the Study of Ethical Problems in Medicine, I believe that the failure of the public and its representatives to explore such an ethical premise fully and to adopt it explicitly is partially responsible for our failure over the past two decades to ameliorate the problem of access. Of course, people with a professional interest and involvement in public policy concerning health care are likely to find the suggestions in this paper fairly agreeable; indeed, many have probably been guided by such precepts, whether or not they stopped to articulate them or to offer a fully developed philosophical justification for them. Nonetheless, even within the health policy community, it seems that attention is focused much more on short-range than on long-range issues; for example, at present, concerns about cost-cutting have crowded out concerns about inequities. Furthermore, when a new program comes in for its first (inevitable) challenges, the absence of a strong philosophical justification for the program (as opposed to the pragmatic justification that it was supposed to solve one or another administrative problem) makes it much more vulnerable to being altered in an unprincipled fashion. Thus the failure to ground policies on a firm ethical footing makes them not only less likely to move society forward toward a goal of a more equitable health care system but, ironically, also more vulnerable to any (frequently self-interested) challenge, which in turn leads to ad hoc changes and a system that even more resembles a patchwork quilt.

This is not to say that practical problems of the moment ought

19

to be ignored. Indeed, efforts to trim health care costs by reducing waste (for example, unnecessary X-rays, tests, or antibiotics) are desirable by any measure.[14] Unless some savings are made in health care expenditures, the public will to address the issue of access is unlikely to materialize. Cost-containment measures are not all equivalent, however; some are likely to worsen access problems, while others might make the system more equitable. The commission looked, for example, at the tax subsidies for health care created by the medical expense deduction and the exemption from employees' taxable income of all contributions by their employers to health insurance plans. This special tax treatment of employment-based insurance adds up to a hidden subsidy for health care that is larger than the federal contribution to Medicaid and almost half the size of Medicare. Further, it is a subsidy that goes disproportionately to those who are better off financially and who have good access to care. A fairly recent proposal by Professor Alain Enthoven has as one of its main objectives a change in the treatment of employment-based insurance. Enthoven cites the unfortunate cost-increasing incentives that the present system provides with its open-ended exemption of all employer contributions to health insurance premiums. He also notes that the revenue lost to the government because of these subsidies is growing much faster than the gross national product and that the system reinforces the link between jobs and insurance. In my view, however, his most significant point is that the distribution of these subsidies is regressive; as he notes, although government now pays about half of the total cost of health care services, "we still do not have universal health insurance."[15] If, as he claims, his proposal would increase the number of people who have coverage, that result is *at least* as important as its effects on consumer behavior or its beneficial effects on the federal deficit.

Of course, the tax subsidy issue is just one example of many issues on the health care reform agenda. In evaluating all proposals for change, one must have ethical as well as economic and scientific objectives clearly in mind.[16]

Health Policy's Relation to "Micro" Ethics

In the preceding section I considered the application of ethical analysis to health policy at the "macro" level. As I observed at the outset, the traditional subject of medical ethics has been the relationship of physician and patient, and I believe that attention at the "micro" level is also important for those concerned about health policy. Plainly, ethical and legal expectations about informed consent, for example, have a direct bearing on the scope of medical care and hence on health costs. To illustrate the general point, I want to focus on one topic in particular.

Policies on Life-Sustaining Treatment. Life-sustaining treatment has long been one of the major areas of concern in medical ethics. When life is at stake, moral views take on a special importance; they are not matters of merely theoretical interest. The President's Commission found that several points on this issue have emerged and enjoy widespread support:

> First, the voluntary choice of a competent and informed patient should determine whether or not life-sustaining therapy will be undertaken. Thus, it becomes very important for health care institutions and professionals to enhance patients' abilities to make decisions on their own behalf and to promote patients' understanding of available options.
>
> Second, health care professionals serve patients best by maintaining a presumption in favor of sustaining life, while recognizing that competent patients are entitled to choose to forgo any treatment.
>
> Third, health care institutions may justifiably restrict the availability of certain options in order to use limited resources more effectively or to enhance equity in their distribution. Such limitations are suspect, however, if they are applied initially or disproportionately to the weakest and most vulnerable members of the population, namely those who are dying—in other words, cost-cutting efforts have to be broadly based.[17]

"No Code" Orders. These—and related—ethically based conclusions have myriad implications for decisions about life support. One particular area with significant implications for health care financing and delivery is cardiopulmonary resuscitation (CPR) of hospitalized patients. Resuscitation capabilities have developed dramatically over the past several decades, but in recent years recognition that uniform policies of "coding" all patients may be ill-advised has been growing. From my perspective, I would describe such reevaluation as ethically based—that is, it proceeds from a recognition that resuscitation is not always in the best interest of every patient. If we think about certain aspects of cardiopulmonary resuscitation, this conclusion is hardly startling:

> First, cardiac arrest occurs at some point in the dying process of every person—so a decision whether or not to attempt resuscitation is potentially relevant to everyone.

Second, without heartbeat, a person will die within a very few minutes.

Third, once the heart has stopped, any delay in resuscitation greatly reduces its efficacy. Hence, a decision about resuscitation ought to be made in advance.

Fourth, resuscitation is helpful to a few patients but not to most—and it can carry substantial risk of morbidity even when "successful."

Fifth, unfortunately, there is no reliable way *during* resuscitation to predict by clinical signs the eventual functional recovery of a patient—usually, one goes on until heartbeat is restored, or it is clear that it cannot be.[18]

These facts have led—over the past ten years or so—to the growing acceptance of "No Code" or "Do Not Resuscitate" (DNR) policies. For example, the American Heart Association and the National Academy of Sciences in their 1974 "Standards for Cardiopulmonary Resuscitation" stated that "CPR is not indicated in certain situations, such as cases of terminal irreversible illness where death is not unexpected."[19]

People involved with health policy, especially those holding responsible positions in institutions and in state and local government, can help develop and implement clear and reasonable DNR policies. They can work with lawyers—including state and local prosecutors—to clarify the law in this area. Basically, the best legal advice I know is twofold. First, orders not to resuscitate are just like other aspects of medical decision making and hence are judged by the same rules (about benefit, consent, and due care) as other types of treatment. Second, an explicit policy, which allows decisions to be made and communicated openly is preferable to no policy or to a policy that drives DNR orders into the nether world of chalkboard notations, pages to be removed from a patient's chart, disappearing ink, or other such childish devices. Yet, despite this straightforward approach, one must acknowledge that there is some legal confusion related to DNR orders, particularly regarding medical decisions about incompetent patients (where withdrawal of treatment would result in death).

Perhaps even more important than these legal concerns in protecting the interests of patients and their families, hospitals and nursing homes should have explicit policies and procedures on orders not to resuscitate. Such policies should include several features:

- They should require that DNR orders be written.
- They should delineate who has the authority to write such orders and to stop a resuscitation effort in progress.

- They should provide for a means of internal review.
- They should give guidance on when, if ever, it is acceptable not to discuss the DNR issue with a patient or next of kin and when a DNR order may be written without explicit sanction by a patient.

The potential confusion about the meaning of DNR orders serves as a reminder that those who come to the ethical issues from a financing and planning side not misunderstand the clinical situation. For example, it will frequently be appropriate to expend significant efforts to treat a seriously ill patient, while still accepting a "no code," should those efforts prove unable to stem the collapse of the multi-organ system, including cardiac arrest.

Improved Quality of Decisions. Health policy analysts can encourage local efforts to improve the quality of life-and-death decisions in institutions in their state. Physicians are becoming increasingly willing to seek advice and to share decisions as they realize both the limits of their own expertise—especially on a subject where values and personal objectives can differ so much—and their legal risks from poor decisions.

With the Baby Doe regulations, the federal government has injected itself forcefully into this area, and there is no reason to think its efforts will stop with infants, since the Rehabilitation Act of 1973 could be applied just as well to any seriously ill patient. The President's Commission did not find the resulting adversary atmosphere conducive to good medical decision making. The commission preferred to see improvements in local decision making—for example, to see health care institutions try out various forms of ethics committees that would draw on more than just physicians and nurses and would aim to clarify the ethical issues involved in such cases and help all participants to understand what is at stake and why. The experience of the relatively few hospitals that have had such committees is that many so-called ethical dilemmas and disagreements are simply instances of poor communication.

The point of these illustrations is that the gulf between the traditional concerns of medical ethics (now "bioethics") and of health policy and planning can no longer be allowed to remain unbridged. Policies and practices at the clinical level have implications that are too important for the financing and delivery systems to be relegated to a separate sphere. People involved in health care policy will need to participate increasingly in the dialogue about such subjects, to which they can bring their broader perspective and from which they can learn a great deal of immediate relevance to their own decisions about the allocation of scarce resources.

Notes

1. *N.Y. Times,* December 25, 1983.

2. 42 U.S.C. §300v-1(a) (1)(D) (Supp. 1981).

3. President's Commission for the Study of Ethical Problems in Medicine and Biomedical and Behavioral Research, *Securing Access to Health Care* (1983), pp. 92–95.

4. President's Commission on the Health Needs of the Nation, *Report* (1953), p. 3. In a similar vein, Daniel Callahan has observed:

> Two slogans, the "right to health" and the "right to health care," encapsulate the thinking that has recently dominated medicine in this country. . . .
>
> The slogans about rights provide the ideological and political ground on which to lay the foundation for some other solution to the distribution of medical care. But the language of "rights" is notoriously slippery, not only because opinions differ regarding their nature and basis but also because rights that are claimed are not all compatible or consistent with one another.

"Health and Society: Some Ethical Imperatives," in J. H. Knowles, ed., *Doing Better and Feeling Worse* (N.Y.: W. W. Norton & Co., Inc., 1977), pp. 23, 30.

5. See, for example, Schweiker v. Gray Panthers, 453 U.S. 1 (1981), which holds that resources are to be "deemed" available to beneficiary when determining eligibility.

6. This is usually the case with so-called positive rights, that is, when X is free to demand something from Y, then Y has an obligation to provide it; the obligations that flow from negative rights—that is, freedom from something—are harder to attach to a particular person and may be said to apply to the world at large, for example, the obligation of everyone to respect a person's privacy.

7. *Securing Access to Health Care,* p. 18.

8. Ibid., p. 19.

9. Ibid., p. 20.

10. Ibid., p. 39. Indeed, practitioners are frequently unaware of the costs of many of the tests and procedures they order. See, for example, L. R. Kirkland, "The Physician and Cost Containment," *JAMA*, vol. 242 (1979), p. 1032; S. J. Dresnick et al., "The Physician's Role in the Cost-Containment Problem," *JAMA*, vol. 241 (1979), p. 1606; S. P. Kelly, "Physicians' Knowledge of Hospital Costs," *Journal of Family Practice*, vol. 6 (1978), p. 171.

11. U.S. Congress, House, Committee on Science and Technology, *Organ Transplants, Hearings before the Subcommittee on Investigation and Oversight*, 98th Congress, 1st session, April 13, 14, and 27, 1983.

12. Proposals have been made to revive the assessment process in new guises. John Iglehart, "Another Chance for Technology Assessment," *New England Journal of Medicine*, vol. 309 (1983), p. 509.

13. See, for example, Thomas W. Moloney and David E. Rogers, "Medical Technology—A Different View of the Contentious Debate over Costs," *New England Journal of Medicine*, vol. 301 (1979), p. 1413.

14. Research on cost-containment does, however, raise novel ethical problems of its own.

15. Alain Enthoven, "A New Proposal to Reform the Tax Treatment of Health Insurance," *Health Affairs*, vol. 3 (Spring 1984), pp. 21, 28.

16. In a recent review of *The Sick Citadel* by Irving J. Lewis and Cecil G. Sheps, Dr. James F. Fries of Stanford Medical School writes that "Public policy for health care . . . is traced from humble 19th century beginnings to a present scientific imperative based upon proven bioscientific knowledge and tempered only slightly by concerns about equity and cost." *Science*, vol. 224 (1984), p. 710.

17. See generally, President's Commission for the Study of Ethical Problems in Medicine and Biomedical and Behavioral Research, *Deciding to Forgo Life-Sustaining Treatment* (1983), pp. 43–90.

18. See ibid., pp. 235–36.

19. American Heart Association-National Research Council/National Academy of Sciences, "In Support of Life, Standards for Cardiopulmonary Resuscitation (CPR) and Emergency Cardiac Care (ECC)," *JAMA* (supp.), vol. 227 (1974), p. 833.

2

Financing Care for the Poor and Underinsured: An Overview

Marion Ein Lewin

Dramatic change and restructuring in the health care marketplace have catapulted to the center of public policy attention the issue of financing care for the medically indigent—persons without health insurance coverage or other resources to pay for needed health care services. Many of the supports and cross-subsidies that have in the past helped cover the costs of indigents' health care have been eroded in this era of funding cutbacks and of growing cost consciousness of purchasers. Heightened competition, altered federal policies, and shrinking national and state budgets have pushed to the forefront the dilemma of the approximately one in ten individuals in this country without insurance and, in many cases, without access to care. There is growing awareness that market-based reforms, so enthusiastically supported in some quarters, cannot succeed over time if they are perceived to disregard the uninsured poor.

Today states and localities, as well as the federal government, are struggling with ways to address the issue of uncompensated care constructively. In searching for practical approaches, however, actors at all levels are acutely aware that potential solutions will not be viable unless, above all, they take into account the current financing and delivery environment for health care. Restricted dollars and the small likelihood—at least in the near future—of new sources of funding highlight the importance of designing strategies that promote efficiency, stretch limited available moneys, and distribute the burden

The author thanks Jack A. Meyer and Jack Needleman for their careful review of this paper and for providing a number of helpful comments and suggestions and Marion C. Strong and Marie Hackbarth for their editing and support assistance.

26

of financing indigent care more equitably among public and private payers. This paper will review dimensions of the uncompensated care issue and describe several programs that have been implemented or are being developed in the attempt to ameliorate this pressing public policy concern.

Federal Programs for the Poor

Although several publicly financed efforts directed at care for the underserved are in place, Medicaid is by far the largest health program for the poor. Title XIX extends health care services to more than 21 million recipients and pays for more than 11 percent of all personal medical services in the United States, including 10 percent of all hospital care and more than 50 percent of all nursing home care.[1] In most states, Medicaid represents the largest health budget item; state and local governments' share of Medicaid costs in 1983 totaled $16.2 billion. The federal share of Medicaid spending in 1983 was approximately $19 billion.[2]

Eligibility requirements for Medicaid vary strikingly from state to state. At a minimum, states must cover all persons who receive cash payments from either the Aid to Families with Dependent Children (AFDC) program or the Supplemental Security Income (SSI) program for the aged, blind, and disabled. Eligibility for AFDC— and therefore Medicaid—is determined by complex means tests. Each state establishes a *need standard*, the income it decides is essential for basic consumption items such as food, clothing, shelter, fuel, personal care items, and utilities. The *payment standard* determines the extent to which the state cash assistance program will meet the need for a minimum standard of living. A state meeting less than full need but having a high need standard may, in fact, provide a substantially higher level of assistance than one meeting full need under a lower need standard. Benefits are generally computed by subtracting countable income (excluding certain disregards) from the state's payment standard. As can be seen in figure 2–1, need and payment standards vary widely, reflecting the considerable latitude states are given in determining AFDC need and payment criteria.

States can extend Medicaid coverage without cash assistance to other AFDC-related groups, known as the "optional categorically needy" (OCN), and receive federal matching funds. The OCN categories include groups of individuals who have incomes at or below levels established under welfare programs but who are ineligible for welfare, either because they fall outside federal requirements under the financial assistance programs or because their states maintain

27

FIGURE 2–1

AFDC Need and Payment Standards for Selected States and Percentage of Need Paid, Family of Four with No Countable Income, January 1985

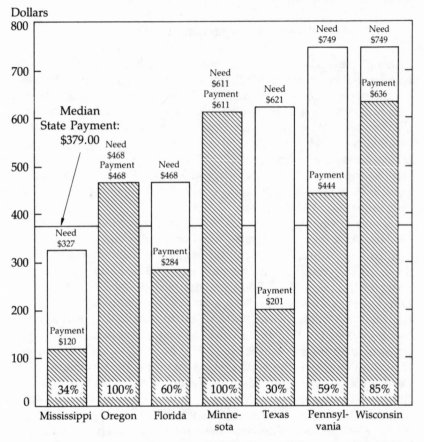

SOURCE: Commission on Ways and Means, U.S. House of Representatives, *Children in Poverty* (May 1985).

very limited cash assistance programs with few eligibility options. Furthermore, thirty-two states have medically needy (MN) programs, an important option under Medicaid, which permit states to accommodate those individuals who meet all criteria for categorically needy assistance, with the exception of income and asset standards, and who have incurred relatively large medical bills. Since 1969 the MN income standard has been limited to 133⅓ percent of the maximum assistance payments for similarly sized families under AFDC in a given state. Through the spend-down provision, persons or families can also become eligible for medical assistance under the MN program if they have an income above the 133⅓ percent range but have high medical expenses that reduce income below the MN maximum. Today almost half of total national Medicaid expenditures pays for services for medically needy and optional recipients.[3]

Although by almost any measure Medicaid has dramatically improved access to medical care for the nation's poor, the program is frequently assailed for several reasons. The wide discretion given to states in determining eligibility, scope of benefits, and payment standards has resulted in inequitable treatment of recipients and those potentially eligible. Entitlement is often more a function of where a person or family resides than that of documented need. Because of Medicaid's categorical nature, many poor and equally needy persons (for example, childless couples, low-income single individuals, and intact families) are ineligible to receive benefits. Approximately half of the nation's poor are not currently covered by Medicaid.

There are other programs supported all or in part by federal dollars that extend health care services to the medically needy. Before the passage of Medicaid in 1965, the government initiated a series of categorical health programs directed at the medically underserved. Many of these efforts focus specifically on improving access to ambulatory care in urban and rural settings. The Community Health Centers (CHCs), the Indian Health Service, the National Health Service Corps, and Maternal and Child Health Programs have been noteworthy both for making available needed health care resources and for providing alternative models for the delivery of primary care to vulnerable target populations.

Under the Hill-Burton Act enacted in 1946, health care facilities, as a condition for receiving construction grants, were obligated to provide assurances that indigent patients would have access to a reasonable volume of uncompensated care. In 1979 this obligation was spelled out more specifically. Institutions receiving Hill-Burton funding were required to provide charity care in an amount equal to 10 percent of the original grant or 3 percent of operating costs, minus Medicaid and Medicare—whichever is less—each year. Estimates are that Hill-Burton facilities are currently obligated to deliver a total of $5 million of charity care annually.[4] The overall effectiveness of Hill-Burton in meeting hospital-based charity care needs has frequently been questioned: interpretations of the law differ, and compliance with the record-keeping requirements under the program has been spotty. Overseeing the program has been difficult.

29

State Programs

Using various approaches, states attempt to close some of the gaps left by Medicaid. The following are examples of approaches used:[5]

• *Medical Indigency Programs.* Many states operate, at either the state or local level, provider reimbursement programs for certain low-income populations not eligible for Medicaid or other federally supported programs. Coverage may extend only to cash assistance recipients or to those with income and resources sufficient to meet daily needs but not medical expenses. Although several states extend Medicaid coverage to the "noncategorically needy" using state-only dollars, others choose to cover more limited benefits. A few states and localities offer only emergency and acute care, and some county programs make benefit decisions on a case-by-case discretionary basis. Unlike Medicaid, a state or county medical indigency program can target the specific population and services covered. States can limit their overall budget outlays by setting appropriations ceilings or low rates for provider payment.

• *Programs for Specified Medical Conditions.* Some states and counties provide funds for low-income individuals with certain medical conditions, such as neonatal intensive care patients, crippled children, and shock-trauma and burn cases. Although eligibility is usually determined on a means-tested basis, not everyone who is eligible obtains services under these programs. Many state programs for special medical conditions receive some level of federal funding.

• *State Catastrophic Expense Programs.* Alaska, Rhode Island, Maine, and, formerly, Minnesota have instituted programs that cover populations for serious and expensive illnesses and often benefit low-income and uninsured persons. A Congressional Budget Office study of catastrophic medical expenses found that over a three-year period, 5 percent of families experienced total expenses in excess of $10,000 in one of the three years.[6] Although the population served by catastrophic coverage is generally small—approximately 2 to 3 percent of the total population—states that have implemented such programs have seen their costs rise rapidly. In Rhode Island, for example, program expenditures grew from less than $1 million in 1976 to $2.5 million in 1982.

• *Direct Provision/Subsidization of Services.* Most states or local governments operate or support public hospitals, clinics, health centers, and related programs that serve the poor and uninsured. Local governments frequently provide lump sum payments to such public facilities but maintain considerable influence over the type and level of services offered, access, and provider selection.

Private and Public/Private Programs

Any discussion about sources of financing for the nation's poor, uninsured, and underinsured must not overlook private and public/private programs designed to improve benefit packages or to enhance coverage. State risk-sharing pools, for example, expand access to affordable health insurance through a broader pooling of existing funds. Connecticut, Minnesota, Wisconsin, Indiana, North Dakota, and Florida have programs that provide health insurance to high-risk—though not necessarily poor—persons who cannot otherwise obtain coverage. Similarly, the Multiple Employer Trusts (METs), which have been developed in various parts of the country over recent years, enable self-employed and small business owners with no or very limited insurance plans to purchase more comprehensive, affordable coverage on a pooled basis. Small businesses provide an estimated 56 percent of the private sector jobs in this country.[7]

Hawaii represents yet another private sector approach to enhancing the access to care and the level of insurance coverage. Through special congressional action, Hawaii has implemented a mandated employer-based insurance program that has reduced, at least in some degree, the number of uninsured and underinsured people. Employee Retirement Income Security Act (ERISA) regulations, however, preclude other states from enacting a program such as Hawaii's.

Project Health, a major demonstration carried out in Multnomah County, Oregon, from 1976 to 1980, legitimized the idea that public and private funding sources could be effectively pooled to purchase mainstream health services for poor and near poor residents. Project Health grew out of a pressing need to improve upon the hospital-centered system of care for the medically indigent in Multnomah County. At its peak, Project Health served 10,000 clients monthly, and 89 percent of those participating in the program were enrolled in comprehensive prepaid plans. Evaluations of Project Health show that providing services for the underinsured poor through managed, capitated delivery arrangements resulted in sizable dollar savings compared with the traditional fee-for-service system.

Private health insurers argue that a major component of funding for indigent care occurs through cost shifting— the indirect "tax" placed on hospital-charge payers by Medicare, Medicaid, and some Blue Cross plans that pay less than a proportionate share of total hospital costs. The Health Insurance Association of America (HIAA) estimates the cost shift in 1983 was about $6.7 billion. The extent of cost shifting is frequently challenged by some who maintain that certain payment differentials and disallowances may be appropriate, justifiable, and prudent purchasing behavior. All agree, however,

31

that cost shifting is a serious problem, one that is exacerbated by current government retrenchment and growing competition.

Defining the Scope of the Problem

Issues surrounding care for the medically indigent appear these days to carry with them a ring of urgency. An increasingly competitive environment for health care, changing federal policies, the advent of a new payment method—diagnosis related groups (DRGs)—for Medicare, and cutbacks in Medicaid have all contributed to a steady reduction in assistance to the poor and uninsured. Some indicators that tell us the problems related to access to care are more serious in the 1980s than in the 1970s follow:

• Medicaid provides coverage to a decreasing number of the poor. In 1983 Title XIX served only 53 percent of the population with incomes below the poverty line; in 1976 it served 65 percent.[8]

• Many states have not adjusted AFDC income levels to account for inflation, a major factor contributing to the decline in the number of poor persons served under Medicaid. A congressional Ways and Means publication demonstrates that from 1970 to 1984, state AFDC benefit levels for a family of four, in constant dollars, failed to keep up with inflation in all but two states—Wisconsin and California. Across the country, the median decline in benefit levels over this period, adjusted for inflation, was 33 percent.[9]

• A Government Accounting Office (GAO) study estimated that 493,000 families lost their AFDC coverage as a result of changes brought about by the Omnibus Budget Reconciliation Act (OBRA) of 1981.[10] Most of those dropped from the welfare rolls were the working poor who, when they lost AFDC, also became ineligible for Medicaid.

• A Louis Harris poll conducted in 1981 under the auspices of the Robert Wood Johnson Foundation reported that more than 12 percent of U.S. citizens—28 million people—appear to have particularly serious trouble coping with the health care system and obtaining care when they need it. Between 8 and 9 percent of those surveyed reported themselves as uninsured; 5 percent reported themselves as unemployed. The survey showed that one million families had at least one member who needed medical care during the year but did not receive it for financial reasons. This problem was three times as prevalent among uninsured as among insured families.[11]

• Data from the Urban Institute indicate that among the under-65 population the percentage that is uninsured grew from 14.4 percent in March 1980 to 16.0 percent in March 1983.[12] The study, showing a substantial increase in the number of uninsured dependents of insured spouses or parents, confirms what many see as a growing trend among small employers to reduce the extent of dependents' coverage in the face of escalating premium costs. Between 1981 and 1982, the number of uninsured adults living with an employed, insured spouse almost doubled.

Clearly certain vulnerable target populations, particularly the working and uninsured poor, are experiencing the most severe impact of diminished funding and cuts in programs. The poor are twice as likely to be uninsured as the middle class and three times as likely as those in upper income groups.[13]

Lack of insurance can represent a major barrier to access to care. Data collected in the 1977 National Medical Care Expenditure Survey (NMCES), which provided extensive information on the health care coverage of the United States population, revealed that the insured population under age 65 received 54 percent more ambulatory care from physicians and 90 percent more hospital care than the uninsured. Given the overall lower health status of the poor—who have been shown to have higher rates of almost all types of illnesses—financial barriers to access take on an added significance. NMCES showed that the uninsured in poor health made only half as many physician visits as those on Medicaid and had 50 percent fewer hospital stays.[14]

Poor pregnant women and children have become increasingly underserved groups in light of recent budget cuts and policy changes. The Children's Defense Fund reports that between 1981 and 1982, 700,000 children were taken off AFDC and Medicaid.[15] The percentage of poor children receiving AFDC and Medicaid is lower today than at any time in the past eight years. Only 52 children of every 100 who are poor receive AFDC; only 73 children of every 100 who are poor receive Medicaid. Recent data suggest that in 1982 infant mortality worsened in at least nine states, a reflection in part of a decline in the number of poor, high-risk women receiving adequate prenatal care.

While the effects of cuts fall most heavily on the disadvantaged, the responsibility for meeting their health care needs falls disproportionately on a minority of hospitals. The Urban Institute, using various data including annual and special American Hospital Association surveys, looked at the 1980 financial status of 463 short-term, general, nonfederal hospitals in the nation's 100 largest cities to obtain a clearer picture of how care for the poor is financed.[16] Among the major conclusions were the following:

• Public hospitals provide a proportionately greater share of care to the poor (Medicaid, bad debt, charity) than private institutions. Public hospitals in the 100 largest cities devoted approximately 40 percent of all care to the poor. This share was more than three times larger than the share of care to the poor in private hospitals.

• Public hospitals provided close to 65 percent of all charity/bad debt care—care for which there is not direct third-party coverage.

• In the 100 largest cities, private insurance, Medicare, and Blue Cross account for roughly 80 percent of the financing for private hospitals; for public institutions these payers account for only 50 percent.

• Among private hospitals, the amount of charity care per hospital clearly increased with teaching status. In contrast, public teaching and nonteaching hospitals provide a similar volume of charity care according to the Urban Institute data.

• Public hospitals are significantly more dependent on state and local subsidies than are private institutions.

The Urban Institute analysis indicates that hospitals providing a significant amount of charity care are not automatically financially distressed. Financial stress comes about in large part when institutions, serving primarily Medicaid and Medicare patients, find themselves unable to shift unreimbursed expenditures to other payers, as these hospitals have proportionately smaller numbers of privately insured patients. Hospitals in stress also provide much more outpatient services than institutions on sounder financial footing.

A recent paper by Frank Sloan points out that a hospital's facility mix can have an important and independent effect on an institution's charity care burden.[17] Hospitals with high percentages of beds dedicated to obstetrics, neonatal intensive and intermediate care, and burn care have high amounts of uncompensated care on average. The Sloan paper also suggests that institutions with high percentages of revenue billed to "self-pay" patients have relatively high amounts of uncompensated care.

There is evidence that nonpublic hospitals, both proprietary and nonprofit, are willing to provide a limited amount—a "prudent ratio"— of free care. Beyond that set amount—usually 2 to 4 percent of an institution's overall patient care revenues and varying among the proprietary and nonprofit—hospitals seek ways of limiting their exposure in this area. As the problem of uncompensated care has become more severe, the responsibility for treating the poor and uninsured is shifting more and more to public facilities. In response to these pressures, even public hospitals struggling to survive have begun to institute strategies for cutting their losses and improving their financial status. Some have reduced their staffs or restricted their hours of outpatient and emergency services; others have attempted to limit their Medicaid caseload and increase the number of privately insured patients. Many hospitals have imposed cost sharing or deductible requirements.

The consequences of all these changes and new dynamics in health care delivery and financing have only begun to be assessed. Some preliminary observations can be made, however. Many of the studies and analyses that have begun to provide us with insights into the problems of the poor and uninsured are based on 1979, 1980, and 1981 data and, therefore, have been unable to measure the full extent of changes brought about by OBRA and the impact of the more serious unemployment and economic recession experienced in some parts of the country in 1982 and 1983. The effects that these studies describe may thus be underestimated.

There is also concern—and growing evidence to support it— that many of those who have lost coverage are simply deferring or forgoing needed medical care. If this trend marks an emerging pattern, the social and economic costs associated with those who are poor and lack access to health care services may be greater than are apparent.[18]

Filling the Gaps

While the search continues for more systematic, targeted approaches to financing care for the uncovered, both the public and private sectors are undertaking various efforts to fill in some of the gaps.

Indigent-Care Pools. Among the states, hospital rate setting has achieved renewed popularity, both for its potential to slow hospital cost escalation and for the opportunity it provides for distributing more equitably the burden of uncompensated care among major purchasers. The increasingly prudent purchasing practices of Medicare and Medicaid and payment differentials afforded Blue Cross/ Blue Shield in many parts of the country have aggravated the phenomenon of cost shifting and the consequent burden for charge payers. In recent years, commercial insurers have become leading advocates of state rate-setting programs primarily because of the framework they provide for dealing with price differentials and the financing of care for indigent patients.

New Jersey and Maryland, states with all-payer rate setting programs (prospective pricing systems that apply to all purchasers of health care), include in their rates to hospitals payments for bad debt and charity care, the costs of which are allocated proportionately to all insurers. Institutions receiving such funding must document the exact extent of their need and show evidence of continuing efforts to collect unpaid patient care bills.

Massachusetts, New York, New Jersey, and Maryland, received a waiver from the Department of Health and Human Services (DHHS) allowing Medicaid and Medicare to contribute to a portion of charity care costs. Medicare's contribution is limited to 1.4 percent of total reimbursable costs statewide; Medicaid's participation is extended only to hospitals in which 68 percent of total patient revenues are attributable to Medicare, Medicaid, state and local government subsidies, and uncompensated care. Since the Massachusetts program differentiates between charity care and bad debt—paying for the former and not the latter—the degree of charity care support has been stringently defined to discourage institutions from shifting their bad debt into the charity care column. Because of the way it has been organized, the Massachusetts indigent-care pool benefits primarily a handful of hospitals in the state serving very large numbers of poor and uninsured individuals and may, to some degree, encourage the dumping of uninsured patients by other hospitals onto these institutions.

Whereas the indigent-care financing schemes in New Jersey, Maryland, and Massachusetts are designed mainly to bring about a more equitable payer-mix within hospitals, New York's model and a program being implemented in Florida take a somewhat different approach. Pooling mechanisms in these two states attempt to redistribute dollars among hospitals by shifting money from well-off institutions providing little charity care to those that are financially distressed and serve disproportionately large numbers of poor and underinsured.

New York's all-payer program does not include allowances for bad debt and charity care in the reimbursement schedules set by the state's Office of Health Systems Management. To address this particular problem, a bad-debt/charity-care pool, funded through a tax on all major payers of care and their share of total hospital costs, was established in 1983. Revenues collected are redistributed to hospitals on the basis of the institution's bad-debt/charity-care burden. Although the program is still rather new, it is clear that institutions traditionally serving large numbers of medically indigent have benefited; the pool has shifted some resources from more affluent hospitals to financially distressed institutions.

A question often raised about indigent-care pools is whether such a concept must automatically go hand in hand with all-payer states' rate setting. Can pooling arrangements be implemented in nonregulated states without confronting the problem of private payers passing on the costs of their charity care contribution by raising charges? The tentative answer seems to be affirmative, as seen by recent actions taken by Florida.

The indigent-care pool in that state is financed through a tax on net hospital revenues, which indirectly taxes health benefits. This approach was selected over a tax on insurance because many of Florida's largest employers are self-insured and under the ERISA preemption would not be required to comply with this type of state mandate.

A major rationale behind the development of Florida's pooling strategy is the belief that a more equitable distribution of the bad-debt/charity-care burden among hospitals will allow market-based reforms to succeed and will head off pressures for more wide-ranging regulatory solutions. As part of the overall cost containment strategy, the state is considering a program whereby hospitals will receive incentives to keep their rates of increase within a specified range; outliers would be subjected to increasingly stringent scrutiny and controls.

The Florida pool has a broader financing base than the Massachusetts and New York models; hospital contributions are supplemented by contributions from the state. In addition to being redistributed to hospitals serving significant numbers of medically indigent, money collected will be used to help the state finance an enlarged Medicaid program.

Given current political and budget realities, the pooling concept to finance a portion of indigent care—usually in the form of a tax on health benefits—has gained considerable support. Those who are less in favor of this approach, however, argue that it may help distressed institutions more than it helps the target populations. Health care services for the uninsured poor might well be provided more efficiently and appropriately in prepaid or other managed care settings. At a minimum, funding for indigent care should be linked to incentives for providers to offer, and patients to choose, more cost-effective delivery arrangements.

Medicaid Expansion. A noteworthy development taking place in many sections of the country is the states' renewed interest in some expansion of their Medicaid entitlement to provide benefits to certain needy target populations, in most instances currently uncovered. Although reducing Title XIX expenditures remains a top priority, states in added numbers have begun to realize that cutting Medicaid eligibility and reducing benefits may merely increase the burden of already severely strained state- and county-funded programs in serving the uninsured. The growing number of medically indigent individuals has created an environment in which states find it smart policy to consider discrete, limited additions to Medicaid that bring a sizable inflow of federal matching funds.

In considering Medicaid expansion, however, states want to ensure that counties will continue to shoulder their responsibilities for indigent care. States that are broadening their Medicaid programs are attempting to incorporate into their plans county maintenance of effort requirements to prevent local levels of government from shifting their burdens to the state or to other counties.

In 1981, as an initial response to OBRA, thirty states took at least one action that resulted in reducing or eliminating services, eligibility groups, or provider payments. A 1984 survey of state Medicaid changes conducted by the Intergovernmental Health Policy Project (IHPP), reflected a very different picture. In that year no state adopted the sweeping kind of cuts and restrictions in program eligibility and services that so characterized state programs in 1981 and, to some extent, in 1982. In 1984, seventeen states expanded eligibility; twenty-five states either added a new service or reinstated a previous service which had been cut. [19]

As a result of leeway granted in OBRA, Oregon, Iowa, and South Carolina have established limited MN programs. New and relaxed legal requirements, mandated by P.L. 97–35, now give states the option of implementing MN programs that extend prenatal and delivery services to indigent pregnant women and ambulatory care to children without extending cash assistance and without providing a full-scale MN entitlement to the aged and disabled, who account for by far the greatest proportion of a state's overall Medicaid budget. Florida, as part of a major Medicaid expansion program developed a MN program that will be implemented in 1986. While Mississippi's efforts to establish a limited MN program were unsuccessful, the state broadened coverage for the optional categorically needy. Mississippi estimated that Medicaid coverage for pregnant women and for children would cost the state approximately $4 million, in contrast to the $10 million the state is currently spending to cover the bad debts of hospitals that provide maternity services to disadvantaged and uninsured women. Every dollar Mississippi puts into an expanded Title XIX will be matched by three dollars from the federal government.

Many of the initiatives currently being undertaken by states to broaden Medicaid coverage focus on pregnant women and on children. Not only have these populations been most severely hurt by changes in the AFDC program in the past three years, but many indigent women pregnant with their first child are categorically ineligible to receive Medicaid in several states, as are indigent pregnant women living with their husbands as well as children living with both parents. The cost effectiveness of providing comprehensive prenatal services to these needy, high-risk populations has been well-documented.[20] In recent congressional testimony, a spokesperson for the March of Dimes stated that providing prenatal care to women and children who are not at present receiving it could save $40.7 million a year in neonatal intensive care costs alone.

Many states, while choosing not to expand their Medicaid programs, are looking at ways of spending existing dollars more appropriately and efficaciously. Structural reforms in the organization, financing, and delivery of Medicaid services are being implemented across the country. During 1982, more than two-thirds of the states applied for federal waivers, either to provide home and community-based long-term care services for the elderly and disabled or to direct Medicaid clients to more cost-effective organized systems of care, such as selective contracting, primary care case management networks, brokering arrangements, or HMOs.[21]

As states use their new freedom to implement alternative delivery and financing models, they see the potential of using Medicaid dollars to achieve systemwide cost containment by moving away from the uncontrolled fee-for-service payment structure. The concept of restricting freedom of choice by placing recipients in managed systems of care is being viewed more and more as a way of improving, rather than diminishing their access to high quality, comprehensive medical services. Although many of these new payment and delivery arrangements are still in the development stage, there is already some evidence of their effectiveness. The Michigan Medicaid program, for example, has enrolled 87,000 recipients, primarily from the Wayne County area, in HMOs, using at-risk contracts. Savings for the first year are projected to be about $7 million compared with what Medicaid would have expended in the traditional fee-for-service system.[22] Similarly, Oregon's Multnomah County Project Health demonstration showed that a successful brokerage model offering a choice of prepaid plans could realize significant cost savings.

Federal Initiatives. Although most efforts related to enhancing coverage for the underinsured poor appear to be focused on the states, Congress has undertaken some limited new initiatives in this area as well. For example, the Deficit Reduction Act of 1984 (P.L. 98–369) reversed some of the funding cutbacks that had come with the passage of OBRA. The act enables certain families, who have lost or who might lose AFDC because of limitations on earned income disregards, to maintain eligibility for Medicaid for at least nine months (and at state option, for an additional six months). P.L. 98–369 established a modified child health assurance program (CHAP) that requires states to extend Medicaid coverage to the following groups meeting the AFDC income and resource criteria: first-time pregnant women, married pregnant women in two-parent families where the principal breadwinner is unemployed, and children up to age five living in two-parent families.

Beyond expansion of Medicaid, there has been some discussion in Washington about increasing the federal excise tax on cigarettes and alcohol as revenue sources for indigent care. Putting aside the merits or shortcomings of such a financing strategy, one sees indications that consumption revenues are already being eyed to bring additional dollars into the failing Medicare Hospital Insurance (HI) trust fund. Another option that has been proposed is the development of a block grant program to be used by states to deal with the indigent-care problem. Funds coming to the states would be passed to local governments, which would decide how the money would be spent. Although the block grant approach has much support, current pressures for deficit reduction dim the prospects for passage of such a program at this time.

The issue of the federal role as it relates to individuals who need services but are unable to pay for them often leads to a discussion of existing government subsidies that, some attest, indirectly finance a considerable amount of indigent care. The current preferential tax treatment of employer-based health insurance is widely regarded as a major public subsidy to the private sector—an estimated loss to the government of $26 billion in 1983. The argument is made that shifting some of the costs of unreimbursed care to private purchasers—in other words, private sector support of a perceived public sector responsibility—can be thought of as a reasonable return for the sizable tax advantage the government gives private employers and insurers. Competition advocates point to the advantages of altering to some degree the favorable tax treatment of employment-based insurance, not only for the impetus it provides for consumers to shop more cost effectively for medical care, but also for the opportunity it offers to use some of the dollars saved for more direct financing of indigent care.

Conclusions

Debate continues about the nature and scope of the indigent-care problem—the kinds and numbers of people who are most in need, the extent of the burden on health care institutions, and the appropriate public/private sector responses. There is general consensus, however, that we have entered an era in which growing numbers are being disenfranchised while purchasers are retrenching and the health care system's ability to respond is eroding. Although continued financing of uncompensated care through implicit subsidies appears less and less tenable in today's more competitive health care marketplace, tax revolts on the state level and a federal deficit of more than $200 billion make chances for enlarged public commitments in this area minimal at best. The challenge, then, is to find viable alternatives, more equitable to providers and consumers, for using limited available dollars more efficiently in extending services to the poor and uninsured.

Lacking federal leadership in this area, states are fashioning their own responses. A 1984 survey by the National Conference of State Legislatures indicated that twenty-five states were considering bills to extend coverage of the poor and uninsured.[23] According to the IHPP, eleven states established new mandates to improve access to care for the medically indigent.[24]

In the short term, state-mandated rate setting has attracted support as a way of holding down hospital expenditures and spreading the burden of uncompensated care. There is some concern, however, that in the long term regulatory solutions may not reduce overall health care costs and may thwart the more competitive, market-based reform strategies such as HMOs, PPOs, and other prudent purchasing type arrangements.

It will be in the best interest of public policy to ensure that measures currently being adopted across the country to address the indigent-care dilemma—frequently in a crisis-like atmosphere—do not derail some of the broader reform objectives that the health care system is trying to achieve.

Notes

1. Health Care Financing Administration, *The Medicare and Medicaid Databook* (Washington, D.C.: U.S. Department of Health and Human Services, 1984).

2. Executive Office of the President, Office of Management and Budget,

Budget of the United States Government FY 1985 (Washington, D.C.: U.S. Government Printing Office, 1984).

3. HCFA, *The Medicare and Medicaid Databook.*

4. Conversation with Florence Fiore, Director, Office of Health Facilities, Rockville, Maryland.

5. Timothy J. Eckels and Robert A. Derzon, "Financing Health Care for the Uninsured Poor: State and Local Programs," mimeographed (Washington, D.C.: Lewin & Associates, July 1983).

6. Daniel Koretz, *Catastrophic Medical Expenses: Patterns in the Non-Elderly, Non-Poor Population* (Washington, D.C.: Congressional Budget Office, 1982).

7. James D. McKevitt, "Providing Health Coverage Is a Growing Problem for Small Business," *Business and Health,* vol. 1 (November 1983), p. 40.

8. La Jolla Management Corporation, *Analysis of State Medicaid Program Characteristics, 1983* (Prepared for the Health Care Financing Administration, U.S. Department of Health and Human Services, Washington, D.C., 1983).

9. Background material and data on programs within the jurisdiction of the Committee on Ways and Means, U.S. House of Representatives, February 21, 1984.

10. *An Evaluation of the 1981 AFDC Changes: Initial Analyses* (Washington, D.C.: U.S. General Accounting Office, April 2, 1984).

11. *Updated Report on Access to Health Care for the American People* (Princeton, N.J.: The Robert Wood Johnson Foundation, 1983).

12. Katherine Swartz, *Selected Information about the Uninsured Population under 65 Years Old in 1979, 1981, and 1982* (Washington, D.C.: The Urban Institute, 1984).

13. Karen Davis and Diane Rowland, "Uninsured and Underserved: Inequities in Health Care in the U.S.," *Milbank Memorial Fund Quarterly,* vol. 61 (Spring 1983), pp. 149–76.

14. Gail Wilensky and Marc Berk, *The Health Care of the Poor and the Role of Medicaid* (Hyattsville, Md.: National Center for Health Services Research, 1982).

15. Sarah Rosenbaum, *Children and Federal Health Care Cuts* (Washington, D.C.: Childrens' Defense Fund, 1983).

16. Jack Hadley and Judy Feder, *Survey of Medical Care for the Poor and Hospitals' Financial Status* (Washington, D.C.: The Urban Institute, 1982 and 1983).

17. Frank A. Sloan, Joseph Valvona, and Ross Mullner, "Identifying the Issues: A Statistical Profile," (Paper delivered at "Uncompensated Hospital Care," a symposium at Vanderbilt University, Nashville, Tenn., April 6–7, 1984).

18. Robert J. Blendon and David E. Rogers, "Cutting Medical Care Costs," *JAMA,* vol. 250, no. 14 (October 14, 1983), pp. 1880–85.

19. Intergovernmental Health Policy Project, *Recent and Proposed Changes*

in State Medicaid Programs: A 50 State Survey (Washington, D.C.: George Washington University, June 1985).

20. Rosenbaum, *Children and Federal Health Care Cuts.*

21. Intergovernmental Health Policy Project, *Recent and Proposed Changes in State Medicaid Programs: A 50 State Survey* (Washington, D.C.: George Washington University, December, 1983).

22. Bruce C. Huckaby, "Medicaid Managed Care Programs in Michigan," (Paper delivered at "Changing Social Welfare Policies: An Update of Their Effects on State and Local Programs," a conference at the American Enterprise Institute, Washington, D.C., March 20–21, 1984).

23. *Major Health Issues for the States: 1984* (Denver, Colo.: National Conference of State Legislatures, 1984).

24. Intergovernmental Health Policy Project, *Recent and Proposed Changes in State Medicaid Programs,* June 1985.

3

Recent Changes in Federal Grants and State Budgets

Victor J. Miller

Shifts in the Flow of Federal Funds to State and Local Governments

Federal government intervention in and support for state and local governmental activities grew substantially during the two decades beginning in the late 1950s. Federal grants-in-aid grew from 10.13 percent of state and local spending in 1955 to 26.8 percent at its peak in 1978.

Throughout this period, programmatic growth accelerated first in one area and then in another. Table 3–1 illustrates the ongoing shifts. The creation of the Highway Trust Fund moderated the early dominance of income security programs (Aid to Families with Dependent Children [AFDC], Child Nutrition) by 1960. That distribution changed dramatically during the next decade as segments of the Interstate Highway System were completed and as major pieces of social legislation were passed in health (Medicaid), education (Compensatory Education), and community development (Urban Renewal, Model Cities). By 1977 the passage and funding of additional legislation (General Revenue Sharing, Comprehensive Employment and Training Act [CETA]), combined with the spending growth of existing programs (Medicaid, waste-water treatment construction) continued to reshape the grant landscape. Spending on education, training, employment, and social services (the bulk of the so-called discretionary grants-in-aid for social programs), which had risen from 7 percent of federal grant outlays in 1960 to the dominating position of 27 percent in 1970, maintained a narrow but shrinking dominance.

As federal grants grew, the change in functional composition produced shifts in the geographic distribution of funds. In general,

TABLE 3–1

PERCENTAGE DISTRIBUTION OF FEDERAL GRANTS-IN-AID OUTLAYS
BY FUNCTION, 1957–1985

Function	1957	1960	1967	1970	1977	1980	1983	1984	1985
Energy	a	a	a	a	a	1	1	1	a
Natural resources and environment	1	2	2	2	6	6	4	4	3
Agriculture	9	3	3	4	1	1	2	2	2
Transportation	24	43	27	19	12	14	14	16	18
Community and regional development	1	2	6	5	7	7	5	5	5
Education, training, employment and social services	8	7	25	27	23	24	17	18	17
Health	4	3	10	16	18	17	22	22	23
Income security	49	38	25	24	18	20	27	25	24
General purpose fiscal assistance	3	2	2	2	14	9	7	7	7
Other	1	a	a	1	2	1	1	1	1
Total	100	100	100	100	100	100	100	100	100

NOTE: Detail may not add to total because of rounding.
a. 0.5 percent or less.
SOURCE: Office of Management and Budget Special Analyses of the Budget, various years.

social and community-development programs send a higher proportion of funds to northeastern cities and other areas such as the South where there are concentrations of poverty, while highway and shared-revenue programs send higher proportions to the more thinly populated West.

A combination of events since 1977 has produced significant changes in the number and amount of grants and in their distribution among the states. As table 3–2 shows, grants have steadily declined as a share of the federal budget since federal fiscal year 1977. Not only has the total dollar amount declined, but also the functional distribution of grant funds has changed, shifting the distribution of funds among states. As a result, some states have experienced a sharper decline in federal grant funds than others.

Recent changes in federal grants-in-aid can be attributed to the following: (1) overall cutbacks and changes in structure; (2) the introduction of 1980 Census data into grant-in-aid distributional formulas; (3) variations among the states in economic performance; (4) a deci-

TABLE 3–2

TOTAL GRANTS-IN-AID BUDGET AUTHORITY, 1977–1985
(billions of dollars)

Function	1977	1978	1979	1980	1981	1982	1983	1984[a]	1985[a]
National defense	0.10	0.05	0.09	0.05	0.04	0.11	0.12	0.14	0.16
Energy	0.07	0.38	0.39	0.46	0.42	0.13	0.32	0.31	0.25
Natural resources and environment	2.61	5.45	5.40	4.56	2.53	3.21	3.61	3.52	3.29
Agriculture	0.32	0.45	0.46	0.57	0.83	0.96	1.89	2.06	1.69
Commerce and housing credit	0.02	0.01	[b]	[b]	[b]	[b]	0.06	[b]	[b]
Transportation	4.81	8.20	11.34	12.15	14.32	12.84	18.48	19.28	19.85
Community and regional development	10.21	5.34	5.75	6.32	5.49	4.59	5.69	5.05	4.13
Education, training, employment and social services	23.58	15.39	24.18	21.54	19.95	15.56	17.30	20.45	17.13
Health	12.12	12.64	15.26	16.49	19.35	19.09	15.91	21.85	22.89
Income security	27.83	33.84	26.70	33.62	36.39	28.70	29.59	30.31	25.83
Veterans' benefits and services	0.09	0.09	0.08	0.05	0.06	0.07	0.07	0.08	0.11
Administration of justice	0.58	0.52	0.54	0.41	0.11	0.10	0.10	0.16	0.10
General government	0.17	0.20	0.18	0.23	0.18	0.19	0.19	0.19	0.15
General purpose fiscal assistance	9.21	9.63	8.24	8.55	6.11	6.34	6.29	6.65	6.68
Totals:									
Nominal dollars	91.72	92.19	98.61	105.00	105.78	91.89	99.62	110.05	102.26
1977 dollars	91.72	86.21	85.13	82.24	75.25	61.04	63.32	67.02	59.31
Percent of the budget[c]	19.7	18.4	17.7	15.9	14.7	11.8	11.5	12.1	10.2
By major category:									
Physical resources	18.04	19.83	23.34	24.06	23.59	21.73	30.05	30.22	29.20
Human resources	63.62	61.96	66.22	71.70	75.75	63.42	62.87	72.68	65.96
Other	10.06	10.40	9.05	9.24	6.44	6.74	6.69	7.14	7.09

a. President's budget. b. Less than $5 million. c. Numbers in percent.
SOURCE: "Grants-in-Aid in the FFY 1985 Budget Proposals," *Federal Funds Information for States*, February 1984.

sion by the federal government to focus its aid on physical resource programs; and (5) the effects of energy revenues.

Overall Cutbacks and Changes in Structure. The erosion of congressional Democratic party majorities in 1978 and Republican victories in 1980 created the environment for reducing and restructuring aid. The state government share of General Revenue Sharing payments was the first large program to be eliminated in 1981. Education programs also felt an immediate impact, with already enacted appropriations for 1981 reduced through the rescission process. CETA was first sharply cut back and then eliminated. Further funding reductions in 1982 were accompanied by the most significant restructuring of the grant system in history. Three health block grants and an education block grant were created from groups of former categorical programs; a community development program and another health program were to be phased in; and a small amount of consolidation was achieved with the creation of the Social Services Block Grant. In addition, the Community Services Block Grant removed the direct link between Washington and local community action agencies. Access to entitlement programs for individuals—Medicaid, AFDC, and Child Nutrition—was significantly reduced, as were reimbursements to the states. These changes were designed to limit federal financial exposure and provide the states with the increased flexibility to do more with less. Reduced financial support was to be accompanied by reduced regulation.

Most of the reductions and restructuring were specifically designed to minimize changes in the relative distribution of funds among the states. The one major exception was the education block grant (Chapter 2), which consolidated funding for more than twenty programs. The largest of the consolidated programs, Emergency School Assistance, previously provided the bulk of its funds to large cities in the Northeast and small school districts in the South. The resultant block grant, however, distributed funds on the basis of school-age population (ages 5–17). This distribution especially benefited mountain states such as Utah and Idaho, which have high percentages of young children, at the expense of school districts in the eastern half of the country.

Effects of the 1980 Census. The use of 1980 Census data significantly changed the distribution of funds among states. The 1970 Census and its updates had underestimated both the total U.S. population and its migration out of the Northeast. Since most federal grant-in-aid formulas are affected by population counts—either directly or as the denominator in per capita estimates—the introduction of new data had a major effect on fund distributions. The speed with which the Census Bureau was able to process the data, despite any delays resulting from court challenges or cutbacks in personnel, also had an effect on states' well-being.

The use of 1980 Census data began in fiscal year 1981 in the General Revenue Sharing and Airport Development programs. The revenue loss from General Revenue Sharing grants alone, in the four overcounted regions—New England, Mideast, Great Lakes, and Plains—totaled $38 million in the first year and $69 million in the second.[1]

The manner in which relative processing speed affected the flow of funds can best be illustrated in the Medicaid program. Federal support for state Medicaid programs—the "match"—is a function of a state's per capita personal income in relation to the national average for three preceding years. That match is recalculated every other year. The law required that the amount of the match for federal fiscal years 1982 and 1983 be published in November 1980 based on August 1980 per capita income estimates. When the 1980 Census totals became available in October 1980 and per capita income amounts were reestimated with new denominators, it became clear that many states' new matches would have been significantly different if the new data had been used. The New York match, for example, would not have increased 0.88 percentage points, and the state would not have gained more than $50 million in Medicaid funds for each year. Since per capita income affects the distribution of funds in many programs—AFDC, General Revenue Sharing, National School Lunch, Vocational Rehabilitation, Vocational Education, and others—the impact was substantial.

The introduction of the new data coincided with the cutbacks and restructuring described above, and some agencies were forced to decide whether to introduce the new data in the middle of a fiscal year. Allocations of $3.1 billion for the Social Services Block Grant for fiscal year 1982 were initially made on the basis of 1979 population estimates. When Congress reduced the entitlement level to $2.4 billion after the 1980 Census data became available, the Department of Health and Human Services (DHHS) had to choose between the two sets of population data (1979 or 1980) for the new distributions. In choosing to use the 1980 data for the new allocations, DHHS implicitly aided those states that had been undercounted in the 1979 population estimates.

The use of the new poverty data began in 1983. Those data, which showed significantly higher levels of poverty in the Northeast and lower levels in the Southeast, affected several program appropriations. Although new legislation mitigated the immediate impact of using the 1980 Census data, shifts were substantial by 1984. For example, Compensatory Education grants to five southern states and Alaska fell more than 4 percent below their 1982 levels despite an overall program appropriation increase of 16 percent.

Variations in Economic Performance. Much of federal spending is designed to be countercyclical. That is, it automatically increases macroeconomic stimulus during periods of recession, which in turn falls off during recoveries. These increases are designed to help those individuals and institutions hardest hit to weather the downturns.

Similarly, much grant-in-aid spending is tied to economic conditions. Employment and training funds are distributed among states primarily on the basis of unemployment. Spending for social insurance programs, such as Medicaid, AFDC, and Child Nutrition, automatically increases to reflect the increased numbers of beneficiaries generated by economic downturns.

While the intent of these programs is countercyclical, namely to provide additional economic aid when state economies are depressed, the interstate effect is often the opposite. Because of lags in the data used to distribute funds, those states most in need of support are often penalized. Although the following discussion uses Medicaid funding as an example, the concept can be applied to other programs as well.

The states' shares of Medicaid benefits (vendor payments) currently vary from 50 percent to 22 percent, with the rest being paid by the federal government. That share is based on the ratio of each state's per capita personal income to that of the nation as a whole for three previous fiscal years. This matching rate is recalculated every other year.

The purpose of this formula is to provide proportionately more federal funds to those states with a small tax base; however, the time lag in the data—for example, data for calendar years 1977–1979 were used in calculating the match for fiscal year 1982–1983—often produces results directly opposite from the intent of the legislation. Table 3–3 compares the change in Medicaid matches with changes in employment during the late 1970s and early 1980s. Of the fourteen states that lost employment between 1979 and 1981, six also suffered decreases in their Medicaid match in federal fiscal years 1982/1983 because the match was based on data from 1977–1979, before employment began to decline. Of the remainder, four states continued to receive the federal minimum contribution of 50 percent, and four received increases

TABLE 3–3

CHANGES IN MEDICAID MATCH AND EMPLOYMENT BY STATE, 1979–1987

State	Change in Medicaid Match (percentage points)				Change in Employment (percent)		
	1980/ 1981	1982/ 1983	1984/ 1985	1986/ 1987	1979/ 1981	1981/ 1982	1982/ 1983
Alabama	−1.26	−.19	1.01	.16	−3.49	−1.74	3.75
Alaska	.00	.00	.00	.00	6.02	7.92	8.40
Arizona	.66	−1.60	1.34	.77	9.24	.92	3.82
Arkansas	.00	−.71	1.49	.18	1.40	−1.49	−.32
California	.00	.00	.00	.00	3.52	.33	1.53
Colorado	−.55	−.88	−2.28	.00	6.67	.82	6.13
Connecticut	.00	.00	.00	.00	.41	−.13	1.82
Delaware	.00	.00	.00	.00	1.92	3.02	.37
D.C.	.00	.00	.00	.00	−8.41	−1.41	2.87
Florida	2.39	−1.02	.49	−2.25	8.39	3.52	2.85
Georgia	.94	−.48	1.15	−1.38	4.33	.90	1.59
Hawaii	.00	.00	.00	1.00	8.12	.94	2.79
Idaho	2.12	−.27	1.85	2.11	−2.46	1.01	2.74
Illinois	.00	.00	.00	.00	−.37	−2.90	−.20
Indiana	−.58	−.55	3.20	2.89	−4.18	−3.17	.39
Iowa	4.61	−1.22	−.11	3.66	−2.78	−2.41	.77
Kansas	1.17	−1.02	−1.83	−.67	.35	−2.63	.18
Kentucky	−1.64	−.12	2.77	−.49	.72	−1.44	−.27
Louisiana	−1.63	−1.97	−2.40	−.64	5.20	−1.71	.84
Maine	−.21	1.10	.00	−1.77	1.94	.00	3.39
Maryland	.00	.00	.00	.00	.70	−1.20	3.89
Massachusetts	.13	1.81	−3.43	−.13	1.77	−.11	.65
Michigan	.00	.00	.70	6.09	−5.05	−4.21	2.10
Minnesota	.38	−1.25	−1.72	.74	4.15	−1.87	.05
Mississippi	−.54	−.19	.27	.79	.62	−2.37	−1.58
Missouri	−.30	.02	1.02	−.78	−2.06	−2.06	1.10
Montana	3.18	1.06	−.93	1.97	1.42	.56	.00
Nebraska	4.16	.50	−.99	−.02	.81	−.54	.27
Nevada	.00	.00	.00	.00	13.16	.93	1.15
New Hampshire	−1.74	−1.70	.04	−4.53	2.93	−1.53	5.78
New Jersey	.00	.00	.00	.00	.21	−.72	2.28
New Mexico	−2.81	−1.84	2.20	−.45	3.28	.93	.92
New York	.00	.88	−.88	.00	−.51	−1.14	.90
North Carolina	−.17	.17	1.73	−.36	2.74	−1.98	.19
North Dakota	10.73	.67	−.79	−6.20	2.07	.34	.67

(Table continues)

TABLE 3–3 (continued)

Changes in Medicaid Match and Employment by State, 1979–1987

State	Change in Medicaid Match (percentage points)				Change in Employment (percent)		
	1980/ 1981	1982/ 1983	1984/ 1985	1986/ 1987	1979/ 1981	1981/ 1982	1982/ 1983
Ohio	−.36	.00	.34	2.86	−3.19	−2.87	.31
Oklahoma	−1.78	−3.73	−1.44	−.87	10.18	.36	.29
Oregon	−1.63	−2.85	4.31	4.42	4.23	−2.98	1.79
Pennsylvania	.03	1.64	−.74	.68	.72	−2.71	−.59
Rhode Island	.81	−.04	.40	−1.84	1.85	−2.27	1.62
South Carolina	−.96	−.20	2.74	−.81	−.53	2.06	−.52
South Dakota	4.98	−.59	.12	−.49	−1.54	−2.19	.64
Tennessee	.55	−.90	2.13	−.46	.21	−2.44	2.98
Texas	−2.31	−2.60	−1.38	−.81	7.87	2.42	2.24
Utah	−.91	.57	2.20	1.78	4.30	2.81	.64
Vermont	.38	.19	.78	−2.31	4.68	1.22	.00
Virginia	−.47	.20	−.21	−3.39	1.66	−.04	4.54
Washington	−1.64	.00	.00	.06	.06	−1.55	2.98
West Virginia	−2.81	.60	2.62	.96	−2.49	−5.39	−5.10
Wisconsin	−.58	.07	−1.15	.67	−1.80	−.23	.05
Wyoming	−3.44	.00	.00	.00	11.06	.00	−.41

SOURCES: U.S. Department of Health and Human Services, Health Care Financing Administration; U.S. Department of Labor, Bureau of Labor Statistics; Federal Funds Information for States.

of less than one percentage point. The four largest increases in Medicaid match funds for fiscal years 1982/1983 went to states with increasing employment (Massachusetts, Pennsylvania, Maine, and Montana). Similarly, thirty states lost employment during the 1982 recession, although most regained lost employment during 1983. Nevertheless, nineteen of these states lost Medicaid funds in federal fiscal years 1984/1985 because the Medicaid match for those years was based on 1979–1981 data. Six remained at the minimum, while only five enjoyed increases in their matching rates.

Eleven states are already programmed to lose Medicaid funds during 1986/1987, and thirteen will gain regardless of the performance of their economies. States' matches for federal fiscal years 1986/1987 are displayed in table 3–3. States that are now in the middle of their economic recoveries—Michigan, Oregon, Ohio, Indiana—

can expect to enjoy substantial future increases in Medicaid and AFDC support. All states in the Great Lakes region, except Illinois, will gain substantially. Other states, particularly New England and some farm states, can expect reductions. Regardless of the states' future needs, their federal matching rates for 1986/1987 have been established, based on 1981–1983 data. Table 3–4 illustrates the financial impact of the shift in the matching rates for 1986 by separating the expected change in federal grants into two components—program growth and matching shifts.

A New Federal Focus on Physical Resources Programs. In response to a series of reports on the need to invest in the nation's infrastructure, the federal government has redirected its grant efforts toward physical resources programs, particularly in the area of transportation. The passage of the nickel gas tax in 1982 provided substantial new funds for both highway and mass transit programs. At the same time, the administration proposed full funding for airport development programs. Tables 3–1 and 3–2 highlight the overall redirection of emphasis. Spending for transportation grants in fiscal year 1985 is expected to grow to 18 percent of the budget from a nadir of 12 percent in the late 1970s. This share should increase even further in 1986 and 1987 as the increased authority reflected in table 3–2 spends out.

Table 3–5 highlights the distribution of transportation programs among the states in relation to other grants-in-aid programs. Most Rocky Mountain and Plains states receive greater shares of transportation program funds than they do grants-in-aid funds as a whole. Table 3–6 illustrates this regional comparison. Thus the growth of transportation spending has affected the overall incidence of federal aid distributions.

The Impact of Energy Revenues. Over the past few years variations in energy revenues have also affected grants-in-aid distributions. The distribution of General Revenue Sharing funds is partially determined by state and local tax effort, defined as revenues as a share of personal income. Most energy-rich states have increased their severance taxes in recent years (taxes on minerals taken from the ground). It is not unusual now for a western state to raise more than 20 percent of its tax revenue from such taxes. As a result, General Revenue Sharing allocations to those states have increased, despite level funding for the program overall. For example, Alaska increased its allocation of General Revenue Sharing funds from $13 million to $35 million in three years, whereas Wyoming increased its allocation from $10 million to almost $16 million during the same period. Most states with significant increases in General Revenue Sharing funds during this period—Montana, New Mexico, Oklahoma, Texas, and Utah—also have had high severance taxes. New allocations in 1985 have somewhat reversed this trend, particularly for Alaska, as severance tax and other revenues have declined.

Energy-related dollar flows have also affected shared revenues distributed by the Department of the Interior. Under a series of programs, the federal government earns substantial revenues through commercial exploitation of public lands. Private firms pay the federal government for mining, grazing, and timber harvesting; and a share of the revenues resulting from these leasing arrangements is distributed to the states and counties where the land is located. Under the Mineral Leasing Act, for example, almost $600 million was paid to eligible states in fiscal year 1983.

In reassigning administrative responsibility for the mineral leasing program to the new Minerals Management Service, the Reagan administration also chose to speed up the payments to states. Recipients began receiving monthly rather than semiannual payments in 1984. During fiscal year 1984, recipients received one semiannual payment (covering the last six months of 1983) and eleven monthly payments, resulting in a one-time increase in their payments by approximately $200 million, with the bulk of the funds going to Wyoming, New Mexico, California, Colorado, Utah, Alaska, and Montana.

Summary. The distribution of federal grants-in-aid to state and local governments has changed significantly over the past few years in response to changed levels and emphases within the system and to new data and formulas. Table 3–7 summarizes the shifts, showing that mideastern and southeastern states have lost shares over the past seven years to states in the three western regions. For most states, the largest changes have occurred since the 1980-1981 period. The Great Lakes states, which have increased their share of funds over the seven-year span, nevertheless have lost funds since 1980–1981. The shift in the 1986/1987 Medicaid matching rates is expected to reverse this loss dramatically, increasing the share of future funds going to all states in this region except Illinois.

The Fiscal Condition of State and Local Governments

Analyzing the fiscal condition of state and local governments is always a risky business. State and local governments are not entirely inde-

TABLE 3-4

Projected Effects of the Shift in the Federal Medicaid/AFDC Matching Rate, 1984–1987
(millions of dollars and percent)

	Projected 1986 Grants			Matching Rate (%)			Cause of Change from 1985		
	Medicaid	AFDC	Total	1984/85	1986/87	Change	Match	Program	Total
Alabama	329	53	382	72.14	72.30	0.16	0.8	−22.7	−21.8
Alaska	35	21	55	50.00	50.00	0.00	0	4.1	4.1
Arizona	66	55	120	61.51	62.28	0.77	1.5	12.5	14.0
Arkansas	281	43	324	73.65	73.83	0.18	0.8	19.4	20.2
California	2,129	1,723	3,852	50.00	50.00	0	0	101.4	101.4
Colorado	183	56	239	50.00	50.00	0	0	13.5	13.5
Connecticut	320	116	437	50.00	50.00	0	0	32.6	32.6
Delaware	40	16	56	50.00	50.00	0	0	3.8	3.8
D.C.	167	41	208	50.00	50.00	0	0	2.3	2.3
Florida	698	159	857	58.41	56.16	−2.25	−34.3	163.1	128.8
Georgia	535	176	712	67.43	66.05	−1.38	−14.9	84.5	69.6
Hawaii	84	40	124	50.00	51.00	1.00	2.4	6.3	8.8
Idaho	60	15	74	67.28	69.39	2.11	2.3	6.6	8.9
Illinois	902	436	1,338	50.00	50.00	0	0	25.9	25.9
Indiana	461	101	562	59.93	62.82	2.89	25.8	26.6	52.5
Iowa	230	96	326	55.24	58.90	3.66	20.2	20.2	40.4
Kansas	133	45	178	50.67	50.00	−0.67	−2.4	6.8	4.4
Kentucky	379	104	483	70.72	70.23	−0.49	−3.4	26.4	23.1
Louisiana	566	112	678	64.45	63.81	−0.64	−6.8	67.9	61.1
Maine	179	56	234	70.63	68.86	−1.77	−6.0	19.3	13.3
Maryland	358	136	494	50.00	50.00	0	0	40.9	40.9
Massachusetts	781	216	997	50.13	50.00	−0.13	−2.6	42.1	39.5
Michigan	1,097	644	1,741	50.70	56.79	6.09	186.7	14.2	200.9
Minnesota	610	172	782	52.67	53.41	0.74	10.8	59.6	70.4

State								
Mississippi	315	58	373	77.63	78.42	0.79	3.8	30.3	34.0
Missouri	345	116	460	61.40	60.62	−0.78	−5.9	23.0	17.1
Montana	68	19	87	64.41	66.38	1.97	2.6	3.0	5.6
Nebraska	107	32	139	57.13	57.11	−0.02	0	8.5	8.5
Nevada	39	6	45	50.00	50.00	0	0		0
New Hampshire	75	12	87	59.45	54.92	−4.53	−7.1	6.8	−.3
New Jersey	648	276	924	50.00	50.00	0	0	65.7	65.7
New Mexico	114	36	151	69.39	68.94	−0.45	−1.0	9.8	8.8
New York	4,406	1,076	5,482	50.00	50.00	0	0	505.0	505.0
North Carolina	516	109	625	69.54	69.18	−0.36	−3.3	47.4	44.1
North Dakota	69	10	79	61.32	55.12	−6.20	−8.9	10.0	1.1
Ohio	1,296	410	1,707	55.44	58.30	2.86	83.7	64.8	148.5
Oklahoma	268	49	317	58.47	57.60	−0.87	−4.8	15.9	11.1
Oregon	164	68	232	57.12	61.54	4.42	16.7	12.3	29.0
Pennsylvania	1,141	417	1,558	56.04	56.72	0.68	18.7	44.8	63.5
Rhode Island	159	42	201	58.17	56.33	−1.84	−6.6	12.3	5.8
South Carolina	334	67	401	73.51	72.70	−0.81	−4.5	46.9	42.4
South Dakota	71	14	85	68.31	67.82	−0.49	−0.6	6.0	5.3
Tennessee	492	60	553	70.66	70.20	−0.46	−3.6	22.7	19.1
Texas	1,017	148	1,165	54.37	53.56	−0.81	−17.6	131.6	114.0
Utah	124	39	163	70.84	72.62	1.78	4.0	12.8	16.8
Vermont	71	29	101	69.37	67.06	−2.31	−3.5	4.7	1.3
Virginia	332	90	422	56.53	53.14	−3.39	−26.9	22.9	−4.0
Washington	311	177	488	50.00	50.06	0.06	0.6	32.9	33.5
West Virginia	131	57	188	70.57	71.53	0.96	2.5	9.0	11.6
Wisconsin	674	328	1,003	56.87	57.54	0.67	11.7	58.5	70.1
Wyoming	18	8	27	50.00	50.00	0	0	3.4	3.4
Puerto Rico	59	48	107	50.00	50.00	0	0	−.4	−.4
Territories	5	7	12	50.00	50.00	⌣	0	0	0
Total	23,990	8,440	32,430	N/A	N/A	N/A	231	1,988	2,219

SOURCE: Department of Health and Human Services.

Table 3–5

Distribution of Federal Grant Budget Authority and Change of Total from 1982
(percent)

	Transpor-tation	Education, Training, Employment, and Social Service	Health	Income Security	Other	1984 Total	1982 Total	1982–1984 Change[a]
Alabama	1.49	1.87	1.53	1.44	1.75	1.59	1.57	.02
Alaska	1.02	0.59	0.15	0.44	0.66	0.54	0.55	-.01
Arizona	1.12	1.42	0.39	0.69	0.94	0.88	0.77	.11
Arkansas	0.77	1.02	1.32	0.67	0.89	0.92	0.90	.02
California	9.13	10.31	10.22	11.77	8.24	10.20	10.35	-.15
Colorado	1.29	1.08	0.85	1.10	1.33	1.11	1.11	.00
Connecticut	1.79	1.12	1.29	1.70	0.96	1.41	1.41	.01
Delaware	0.33	0.28	0.18	0.32	0.31	0.28	0.29	-.01
D.C.	1.08	0.69	0.74	0.78	3.42	1.19	1.21	-.02
Florida	3.86	3.61	2.50	2.80	2.69	3.06	2.93	.13
Georgia	2.86	2.18	2.14	2.04	1.86	2.20	2.16	.04
Hawaii	0.82	0.42	0.38	0.43	0.43	0.48	0.48	.00
Idaho	0.53	0.43	0.25	0.24	0.52	0.37	0.34	.03
Illinois	4.62	4.73	4.29	4.78	3.97	4.52	4.68	-.15
Indiana	1.81	2.00	1.92	1.38	1.79	1.74	1.71	.04
Iowa	1.09	1.04	0.89	0.89	1.15	0.99	0.97	.02
Kansas	0.89	0.80	0.66	0.50	0.80	0.70	0.70	.00
Kentucky	1.24	1.57	1.59	1.49	1.73	1.52	1.58	-.06
Louisiana	2.01	1.90	2.14	2.00	1.57	1.95	2.05	-.10
Maine	0.38	0.53	0.74	0.55	0.56	0.56	0.57	-.01
Maryland	2.92	1.60	1.60	1.71	1.58	1.86	2.04	-.18
Massachusetts	2.10	2.43	3.28	3.31	2.40	2.79	3.24	-.45

Michigan	2.75	4.21	4.29	4.36	3.40	3.90	3.91	−.01
Minnesota	1.52	1.51	2.34	1.70	1.65	1.76	1.83	−.07
Mississippi	0.83	1.47	1.19	1.02	1.26	1.14	1.16	−.02
Missouri	1.67	1.85	1.57	1.72	2.01	1.75	1.74	.01
Montana	0.66	0.46	0.32	0.25	0.73	0.45	0.40	.04
Nebraska	0.68	0.59	0.48	0.45	0.58	0.54	0.55	−.01
Nevada	0.48	0.34	0.20	0.18	0.43	0.30	0.29	.01
New Hampshire	0.34	0.34	0.35	0.40	0.41	0.37	0.38	−.01
New Jersey	2.33	2.80	2.80	3.70	2.65	2.95	3.20	−.25
New Mexico	0.61	0.84	0.53	0.42	1.92	0.78	0.69	.08
New York	8.55	8.12	16.80	11.77	8.06	11.02	11.43	−.41
North Carolina	1.71	2.35	2.22	1.97	1.94	2.05	2.01	.04
North Dakota	0.46	0.34	0.30	0.21	0.52	0.34	0.32	.02
Ohio	3.22	4.27	4.86	4.36	3.85	4.18	4.09	.09
Oklahoma	1.16	1.31	1.28	1.06	1.10	1.18	1.18	−.01
Oregon	1.30	1.18	0.76	0.85	1.70	1.10	1.26	−.16
Pennsylvania	4.76	4.75	5.03	5.30	4.78	4.97	5.32	−.35
Rhode Island	0.74	0.44	0.65	0.64	0.42	0.59	0.60	−.01
South Carolina	0.89	1.39	1.26	1.12	1.13	1.16	1.19	−.03
South Dakota	0.47	0.42	0.32	0.23	0.38	0.35	0.34	.01
Tennessee	1.49	1.96	1.82	1.56	2.29	1.78	1.78	.00
Texas	5.67	5.64	4.25	3.65	4.32	4.60	4.25	.35
Utah	0.99	0.65	0.50	0.43	1.04	0.67	0.59	.08
Vermont	0.32	0.29	0.32	0.24	0.30	0.29	0.29	.00
Virginia	2.47	1.96	1.52	1.64	1.72	1.83	1.92	−.09
Washington	2.15	1.79	1.15	1.45	1.43	1.57	1.60	−.03
West Virginia	0.88	0.88	0.58	0.77	1.22	0.83	0.90	−.07
Wisconsin	1.36	1.92	2.82	2.04	1.85	2.03	1.97	.06
Wyoming	0.48	0.26	0.08	0.12	2.28	0.52	0.36	.16
Other and unallocated	5.85	4.08	0.39	5.37	5.09	4.13	2.82	1.31
Total	100.00	100.00	100.00	100.00	100.00	100.00	100.00	.00

NOTE: Detail may not add to totals because of rounding.

a. Change in percentage points.

SOURCE: Data produced by the Federal Funds Information for States System, a joint service of the National Governors' Association and the National Conference of State Legislatures.

TABLE 3–6

1984 Regional Distribution of Federal Grant Budget Authority and Change of Total from 1982

(percent)

	Transportation	Education, Training, Employment, and Social Services	Health	Income Security	Other	1984 Total	1982 Total	1982–1984 Change[a]
New England	5.68	5.14	6.63	6.85	5.05	6.01	6.49	−.48
Mideast	19.96	18.23	27.14	23.58	20.80	22.27	23.49	−1.22
Great Lakes	13.76	17.11	18.18	16.92	14.86	16.37	16.35	.03
Southeast	20.52	22.17	19.81	18.50	20.06	20.05	20.16	−.12
Plains	6.79	6.56	6.55	5.70	7.08	6.43	6.45	−.02
Rocky Mountain	3.96	2.88	2.00	2.14	5.90	3.11	2.81	.30
Southwest	8.57	9.21	6.45	5.82	8.27	7.43	6.90	.53
Far West	13.07	13.62	12.33	14.25	11.80	13.17	13.50	−.33
Alaska	1.02	.59	.15	.44	.66	.54	.55	−.01
Hawaii	.82	.42	.38	.43	.43	.48	.48	.00
Other and Unallocated	5.85	4.08	.39	5.37	5.09	4.13	2.82	1.31
Total	100.00	100.00	100.00	100.00	100.00	100.00	100.00	.00

NOTES: Totals include funding for approximately 200 federal programs constituting 99 percent of the grant-in-aid system. Detail may not add to totals because of rounding.

a. Change in percentage points.

SOURCE: Data produced by the Federal Funds Information for States System, a joint service of the National Governors' Association and the National Conference of State Legislatures.

pendent of the federal government, and a decision by the federal government to slow down payments or to eliminate a program can be disastrous just as a decision to accelerate payments can be a windfall. In addition, though analysts usually focus on operating surpluses and deficits, most governments will tend toward balance: today's deficits will disappear, and surpluses will be absorbed. Measurement problems are exacerbated because we have no current, comprehensive data on spending by the state and local sector. Compared with other sectors of the economy, the Census Bureau collects only annual data on state and local government spending, which are more than a year outdated when first printed. As a result, Department of Commerce current fiscal estimates of the state and local governmental sector are based on anecdotal evidence.

Despite these limitations, most analyses of state and local fiscal conditions rely on the state and local sector of the National Income and Product Accounts (NIPA), published by the Commerce Department. The rationale given is that these data are the only comprehensive source of current information. These data should not be ignored in the analysis. Their limitations should be understood, however, and they should be used only as a supplement to the more relevant data that are becoming available.

State and local governmental activity contributes to the national income, and the Department of Commerce measures that contribution through the state and local sector of the NIPA. This data set is not intended for measuring fiscal condition, however, and the Department of Commerce has discouraged its use for that purpose. Nevertheless, it constitutes the only timely national data available on overall state and local activity, and analysts consistently use it to measure fiscal condition.

At the end of 1983, improving NIPA fiscal margins produced headlines such as "Brightening Prospects for States and Localities."[2] Clearly, the general trend reflected by the NIPA data is correct: the fiscal conditions of state and local governments have improved dramatically from the worst experience in recent history. Nonetheless, in evaluating this improvement the analyst must take into account several factors.

First, the overall measured surpluses reflect primarily these governments' funding of their pension plans. Although funding of the plans obviously has an effect on the flow of funds in the national economy, it has virtually no relevance to the immediate fiscal capacities of subnational governments.

Second, the NIPA figures include capital construction financed through borrowing, usually outside state and local general fund

TABLE 3–7

SHARES OF FEDERAL GRANTS-IN-AID, 1977–1984

State	1977 (%)	1980/81 (%)	1984 (%)	Changes 1977– 1980/81	Changes 1980/81– 1984	Changes 1977– 1984
Alabama	1.70	1.68	1.66	−.01	−.02	−.03
Alaska	.58	.49	.56	−.09	.07	−.02
Arizona	.98	.93	.92	−.05	−.01	−.07
Arkansas	.97	1.00	.96	.03	−.04	−.01
California	10.31	10.28	10.64	−.03	.36	.33
Colorado	1.08	1.10	1.16	.02	.05	.08
Connecticut	1.35	1.28	1.47	−.08	.20	.12
Delaware	.28	.32	.29	.04	−.03	.01
D.C.	1.43	1.50	1.24	.08	−.26	−.18
Florida	3.01	3.13	3.19	.12	.07	.18
Georgia	2.82	2.48	2.30	−.33	−.18	−.52
Hawaii	.61	.50	.51	−.11	.01	−.10
Idaho	.44	.41	.38	−.02	−.03	−.05
Illinois	4.85	4.96	4.72	.12	−.25	−.13
Indiana	1.66	1.82	1.82	.17	.00	.16
Iowa	1.08	1.07	1.03	−.01	−.03	−.05
Kansas	.83	.87	.73	.04	−.14	−.10
Kentucky	1.54	1.59	1.58	.05	.00	.04
Louisiana	1.87	1.80	2.04	−.07	.23	.16
Maine	.62	.58	.58	−.04	.01	−.04
Maryland	1.88	2.04	1.93	.16	−.10	.05
Massachusetts	3.15	3.16	2.91	.01	−.24	−.23
Michigan	4.41	4.39	4.07	−.02	−.32	−.34
Minnesota	1.85	1.88	1.83	.03	−.05	−.02
Mississippi	1.21	1.25	1.19	.04	−.06	−.02
Missouri	1.73	1.84	1.82	.11	−.02	.09
Montana	.53	.51	.47	−.02	−.04	−.06
Nebraska	.56	.58	.56	.02	−.02	.01
Nevada	.31	.38	.32	.06	−.06	.00
New Hampshire	.35	.36	.39	.00	.03	.03
New Jersey	3.33	3.13	3.08	−.20	−.05	−.25
New Mexico	.68	.76	.81	.08	.05	.13
New York	11.27	10.90	11.50	−.37	.60	.23
North Carolina	2.29	2.10	2.13	−.19	.04	−.15
North Dakota	.34	.36	.36	.02	−.01	.02
Ohio	3.80	3.91	4.36	.11	.44	.56
Oklahoma	1.18	1.15	1.23	−.03	.08	.04

(Table continues)

TABLE 3–7 (continued)

SHARES OF FEDERAL GRANTS-IN-AID, 1977–1984

State	1977 (%)	1980/81 (%)	1984 (%)	Changes		
				1977– 1980/81	1980/81– 1984	1977– 1984
Oregon	1.27	1.32	1.14	.05	− .17	− .12
Pennsylvania	5.49	5.14	5.18	− .35	.05	− .31
Rhode Island	.54	.52	.61	− .02	.09	.07
South Carolina	1.21	1.13	1.21	− .08	.08	.00
South Dakota	.36	.44	.36	.07	− .07	.00
Tennessee	1.80	1.97	1.86	.17	− .11	.06
Texas	4.37	4.43	4.80	.06	.37	.43
Utah	.59	.64	.70	.05	.06	.11
Vermont	.34	.35	.30	.01	− .04	− .03
Virginia	1.98	1.99	1.91	.00	− .08	− .07
Washington	1.69	1.88	1.64	.19	− .24	− .05
West Virginia	.96	1.03	.87	.08	− .16	− .08
Wisconsin	2.26	2.36	2.12	.10	− .24	− .14
Wyoming	.28	.34	.54	.06	.20	.26
Total	100.00	100.00	100.00	.00	.00	.00

NOTE: Detail may not add to totals because of rounding.
SOURCES: Federal Aid to States (U.S. Treasury), 1977, 1980; Federal Expenditures by State, 1981; Federal Funds Information for States, 1984.

budgets. Increased capital construction, usually indicating financial health, is reflected as deficit spending, since there is no immediate source of tax revenue to pay for it. In addition, unexpected slow-downs in spending, such as reduced spending on highway construction resulting from the failure of Congress to pass the Interstate Cost Estimate, increase the measured surplus.

Third, the NIPA figures lump state and local governments into one sector. Although the subnational governments are interdependent, looking at the total figures masks differences among regions and among levels of government. A surplus in a large state can mask deficits in many small ones. The substantial increases during the recession in school district and county own-source revenues, often replacing reduced state and federal aid, masked slower increases in state and municipal receipts.

Fourth, NIPA treats all funds similarly, regardless of earmarking and availability. Substantial increases in gas tax revenues are shown as increasing state and local surpluses, even though those funds are earmarked for trust funds in all but five states.

Fifth, the time trend of the data must be carefully observed if it is used to track fiscal condition. For example, many state and local governments ran deficits in their 1982 or 1983 fiscal years, and current surpluses must be used to pay the past debts.

Sixth, and most important, the accounts measure only the financial transactions of government. They do not measure the ability of governments to raise taxes to provide services for their constituents. In a very real sense, the financial condition of a government is determined by its tax base and its levels of debt. Neither of these is reflected in the NIPA calculations.

Taking the above caveats into account, a brief glance at the NIPA figures does give us a general sense of what is happening in the sector overall. Excluding the $30–40 billion annual cash surplus of pension and other social insurance funds, the sector overall fell from small surpluses of $4–6 billion during calendar years 1979–1981 to a deficit of $1 billion in calendar year 1982. It then rebounded strongly in calendar year 1983, with an estimated surplus of $6.6 billion. The 1982 and 1983 figures were reestimated in July based on new data; the Commerce Department had originally estimated a $2 billion deficit in 1982 and a $15 billion surplus in 1983. As expected, the sector adjusted toward balance. The 1983 surpluses, whatever their actual size, are being used to repay previous deficits, restore previous service reductions, accomplish deferred maintenance and employee pay increases, rehire laid-off workers, and reduce temporary tax increases. Part was also dedicated toward rebuilding "rainy-day" funds and other canopies against the coming problems that many state officials expect. Most of the twenty-four state rainy-day funds are of recent vintage. With the exception of funding for prison construction and for elementary and secondary education, few new services were provided without tax increases to pay for them.

The National Conference of State Legislatures periodically surveys legislative fiscal officers in the states, and the results of those surveys are informative.[3] At the beginning of 1984, five states were on a path leading to a budget deficit in their fiscal year 1984. Three of those states—Arizona, Iowa, and Oklahoma—made adjustments to eliminate their projected 1984 deficits. Those states that ended the year with deficits—New Hampshire and Vermont—have since adopted policies to eliminate their deficits during 1985.

In comparison, reports in January 1983 found that nineteen states anticipated deficits for fiscal year 1983. By the end of that fiscal year, action had been taken in eleven of those states, with the result that only eight states ended fiscal year 1983 with deficits.

While these changes parallel those of NIPA, only eight of the states surveyed in September 1984 reported end-of-year surpluses in 1984 in excess of 5 percent of annual appropriations, the amount used by the financial community to measure the financial well-being of a government. The overall $5.3 billion General Fund balance of the surveyed states represented 2.9 percent of total appropriations. Thus the significant turnaround in states' budget deficits reflected both here and in NIPA does not indicate so much financial health for the majority of states but rather the end of a fiscal crisis.

The National Conference of State Legislatures survey, and similar surveys by the National Association of State Budget Officers, indicates that the biggest budget issue of 1984 was the funding of elementary and secondary schools. This subject was a leading budget issue in at least thirty-one states. Fifteen states increased spending for elementary and secondary education by 14 percent or more, with the most significant increases in Tennessee, South Carolina, and Texas. Five states approved substantial sales tax increases in 1982 or 1983 to finance these program enhancements. It is interesting that gubernatorial proposals to increase taxes to pay for improved educational services were defeated in Maryland, New Mexico, and Utah.

Conclusion

During 1982 and 1983, state and local governments went through the worst fiscal crises in the memory of people now active in fiscal affairs. Cutbacks in grants from the federal government were matched by significant reductions in state own-source revenues. As a result, operating surpluses turned into deficits, taxes rose, and services and maintenance were cut back. Few governments anticipated the size or extent of the revenue shortfalls.

Some governments suffered less than others during this period. Energy-rich states generally did not experience revenue reductions during this period, since severance taxes continued to produce high levels of revenues and federal funds were reallocated toward them. Other states, especially those east of the Mississippi, suffered more.

The current improvement in state and local fiscal conditions is not expected to continue, nor will governments see themselves as having much fiscal discretion. To the contrary, state and local governments expected to spend, and did spend, 1984 repairing past damage and anticipating future problems.

Notes

1. See the Federal Funds Information for States, *FFIS Newsletter*, volume I (January 1984), chap. 4, and volume II (October 1984), chap. 2, for further information on revenue-sharing shifts.

2. *The Morgan Guaranty Survey*, October 1983.

3. The ensuing discussion is abstracted from work performed by Steven D. Gold and Corina L. Eckl for the National Conference of State Legislatures.

4

All-Payer Rate Regulation:
An Analysis
of Hospital Response

Douglas Conrad,
Michael Morrisey,
Stephen Shortell,
Michael Chapko,
and Karen Cook

All-payer rate setting for hospitals at the national level, which involves the goverment's establishing and enforcing hospital rates charged to all public and private third-party payers and self-pay patients, was the essential feature of the Carter cost-containment proposal. More recently it was part of the research agenda given to the Department of Health and Human Services as part of the 1983 amendments to the Social Security Act. Many private health insurers are also advocating such a uniform payment system out of fear that hospitals will shift Medicare and other costs to them.

A host of issues attends the development of such a program. A fundamental question is whether all-payer rate setting is the most effective method for controlling health care costs. The answer to that question involves a careful analysis of various options, the trading-off of several objectives, and, at the heart, a judgment as to the appropriate role of government.

In this essay we analyze only one facet of the problem: the likely response of hospitals to the economic incentives inherent in state rate-setting programs. The available empirical evidence provides few estimates of the effects on hospital behavior or cost outcomes of the

Research for this paper was supported by Grant No. HS-03772, Hospital Response to Regulation, from the National Center for Health Services Research. This paper does not necessarily reflect the policy or position of our organizations.

all-payer dimension of rate setting, so the analysis presented here is necessarily based almost entirely on the economic incentives created by the structural characteristics of all-payer rate-setting systems. To draw inferences from such data, one must account for other key elements of rate regulation and for the market conditions that together shape hospital behavior.

The paper proceeds in three steps. First, it discusses the components of rate regulation that we believe significantly determine the nature and the magnitude of the impact on hospital behavior. Second, it presents a brief overview of four all-payer rate-setting systems. Finally, it develops a series of qualitative predictions regarding the behavioral responses of hospitals to all-payer rate regulation.

Significant Elements of Rate Regulation

Our research,[1] as well as that of others,[2] suggests several particularly salient features of rate regulation for predicting the form and degree of effect on hospitals. These features can be characterized as the scope, the restrictiveness, the uncertainty, and the coordination of the program. Scope refers to the unit of revenue controlled, the payers covered, and the extent to which hospital responses are constrained. Restrictiveness refers to the duration of the program and the level of enforcement. Uncertainty refers to the clarity with which the program differentiates constrained and unconstrained behavior. Coordination refers to the integration of rate regulation with other hospital controls, particularly certificates of need. Each of the elements of rate setting provides important incentives for hospital response.

The unit of revenue controlled by the rate-setting program influences the use of the institution and the services offered by the hospital. For example, it is well known that revenue-per-diem programs provide incentives for increased length of stay. Recognition of this response led to the inclusion of length-of-stay limits in the New York rate-setting program in 1976. Alternatively, per-case programs—such as the diagnostic related group (DRG)–based reimbursement mechanism recently implemented by Medicare, the New Jersey DRG experiment, and the Maryland guaranteed inpatient revenue per case (GIR) system—encourage reductions in length of stay and use of ancillary services and also favor admission strategies tilted toward the selection of less severely ill patients. Regulatory constraints directed exclusively at charges for specific services provide a targeted control on the level of prices and the rate of hospital price inflation over time but do not by themselves address utilization, service-mix, or case-mix changes that may result. Total revenue programs offer the greatest potential for regulatory constraint in hospital costs because they place a global limit on revenues but give the hospital unlimited flexibility in satisfying the revenue constraint. They too, however, provide implicit incentives to eliminate services or patients that are relatively more costly to treat. Legislatures have often recognized the multiplicity of objectives by building into the enabling legislation goals that conflict with cost containment but that may serve to limit undesirable outcomes. The condition that the full financial require-ments of hospitals be provided is such an example.

The locus of authority for the rate-setting program can be thought of as an element of restrictiveness. Three approaches are common: the independent commission, the centralized state agency, and private voluntary organizations. None of these inherently ensures a binding or equitable rate-setting program, but different models do suggest different emphases in the implementation of rate regulation.[3] For example, programs administered by centralized state agencies accountable for Medicaid expenditures have strong financial incen-tives to contain hospital reimbursement while, at the other extreme, private voluntary programs are likely to apply rate controls in a more lenient fashion. The independent commission may represent an intermediate case, having less potential for bias (for example, in favor of constraining Medicaid payments to the detriment of other payers) in its implementation of rate regulations and a correspondingly smaller and less concentrated stake in containing hospital costs and revenues.

The method for enforcing compliance with rate-setting constraints is also crucial to program effectiveness. For present purposes, one can distinguish two types of regulatory compliance.[4] First, with static compliance a one-time penalty to next year's revenue is imposed on hospitals whose revenues exceed their allowed level in the rate year. Since subsequent rates are based typically on inflation-adjusted actual costs in the previous rate year, however, hospitals have a short-run incentive to raise actual costs in the base year to increase their allowed rates in future years. The gain, of course, depends upon the size of the penalty, the frequency of payment, and the opportunity cost of capital. In contrast, programs that enforce dynamic compliance base the determination of rates in future years on approved costs in the base year, thus removing the hospital's incentive to inflate costs in the base year.

The use of interhospital comparisons critically affects both the efficiency and the equity of the rate-setting controls. At one extreme, treating each hospital as unique reduces the rigor of the rate or revenue constraint but ensures that different situations are treated differently. As the number of peer groups used for interhospital comparisons increases, the rate-setting program approaches, in effect, a hospital-specific constraint. If a more standardized, formula-based review process were employed by the rate-setting body, such a hospital-specific constraint might achieve maximum equity among hospitals, other regulatory features being equal. If the review process were a highly individualized negotiated agreement between the rate-setting body and hospitals, however, the use of screens based on interhospital comparisons would be important in maintaining equity among hospitals. At the opposite extreme, in terms of interhospital comparisons, the use of a minimum number of peer groups and the application of market-based norms in setting rates together might contribute to the stringency of the regulatory constraint and provide stronger incentives for relatively inefficient hospitals to reduce their costs. Since there are legitimate differences among hospitals in the nature of their product and the complexity of case mix, however, the use of market averages does not automatically provide stronger relative incentives for efficiency. Reimbursement mechanisms based on case mix, with the appropriate adjustments for case severity, arguably offer the best selective incentives for hospital efficiency.

The other principal regulatory program with which state rate-setting systems coordinate their cost-containment activities is the certificate-of-need (CON) authority. Among the current all-payer state rate-setting programs, Massachusetts treats CON-approved capital expenditures as pass-throughs in setting the allowable rate base, while Maryland, New Jersey, and New York independently apply capital cost and operating cost screening criteria to all projects irrespective of their CON approval status.[5] Another critical dimension of linkage to CON is the enforcement by the rate-setting program of the hospital's rate projections within its CON application when allowable revenues are determined for the individual hospital. This kind of enforcement mechanism reinforces the rigor of CON constraints in capital expenditure.

Description of Current All-Payer Rate-Setting Models

Maryland. The rate-setting program currently in effect in Maryland comprises three approaches: rate review, inflation adjustment, and the GIR (per case) system. Under the rate review system all hospitals are required to submit annual data on base and budgeted years. Total approved revenues have four components: direct and allocated indirect departmental expenses; other financial considerations (for example, bad debt, charity care, and working capital allowances); a payer differential; and a capital facilities allowance for buildings and equipment. These components, as approved by the Health Services Cost Review Commission, are used to develop an initial set of rates per unit of service by revenue center.

The rate review system is applied relatively infrequently since most hospitals now receive rate increases under the inflation adjustment system (IAS). The IAS adjusts allowable revenues for market (exogenous) increases in input prices, for the variable cost portion of unanticipated volume changes, for changes in case and payer mix, and for certain pass-through costs (costs mandated by state or federal government, such as minimum wage increases and increases in costs beyond the Consumer Price Index in the hospital sector). The GIR system sets an average charge for each diagnosis (based on DRGs) for each type of payer, and as of May 1982 has been in effect for twenty-one hospitals (including all hospitals with at least 400 beds). The characteristics of the Maryland system are summarized in table 4–1.

New Jersey. The New Jersey program is unique among state rate-setting models in that it is the only one to date that covers all payers under case-mix-based reimbursement. New Jersey's experience with prospective payment by DRG, therefore, provides a natural experiment with respect to the effect on hospital behavior of reimbursement based on case mix within an all-payer system. Since now so few other all-payer states exist and since the effects of scope of payers covered and unit of revenue controlled may be dependent on one another, separating the effect of those two features of rate regulation is difficult. For example, a total revenue constraint is more likely to be effective in a program that covers all payers, thereby foreclosing potential cross-subsidization by payer in the form of rate increases to uncovered payers.

We focus on the per case characteristics of New Jersey's rate-setting system because that element of the regulatory model implies several side observations about the workings of an all-payer system. First, in a program that controls all payers, the potential for hospital cross-subsidies shifts from payers to services. Under an all-payer rate-setting program, if neither total revenues nor revenue per case is controlled, the hospital might potentially gain (for example, under a charge-based system) by repricing services with less elastic (price-sensitive) demand or by increasing the volume of activity for more profitable services. The revenue per case constraint removes this incentive for cross-subsidization by service and replaces it with a potential gain from selecting more profitable case types.

TABLE 4-1

CHARACTERISTICS OF ALL-PAYER RATE-SETTING PROGRAMS

	Unit of Revenue	Locus of Authority	Type of Compliance	Coordination with Other Regulatory Programs	Use of Interhospital Comparison
Maryland	Total revenue, departmental revenue, guaranteed revenue per case (GIR)	Independent commission (HSCRC)	Static, rate-year only	Not automatic with certificate of need (CON), rate-setting provides input to CON	Extensive, use of budget with screens
New Jersey	Revenue per case (DRG, or diagnosis-related group)	State Department of Health, New Jersey Hospital Rate-Setting Commission	Static, rate-year only	Not automatic, input	Extensive, use of budget with screens

(handwritten notes, Maryland row): LOTS OF AUTHORITY (BUDGET) → BOTTOM LINE IS REVIEWED

(handwritten notes, New Jersey row): → NO AUTHORITY → REVIEWED ON CASE BY CASE BASIS.

New York	Per diem, (DPM) charges	State Department of Health	Some dynamic compliance incentives, constant base over three-year period for rolling forward allowed rates in subsequent years	Not automatic, input	Extensive use of peer group ceilings, coupled with minimum utilization requirements and case-mix adjusted length of stay (LOS) standard
Massachusetts	Charges, percent of approved budget, per diem (MAC)	Massachusetts Rate-Setting Commission	Dynamic compliance maximum allowable cost (MAC) limits	Automatic, input denies reimbursement for unapproved projects	Limited, hospital-specific maximum allowable cost caps, rolling forward hospital's base year costs

SOURCE: Craig Coelen et al., *First Annual Report of the National Hospital Rate-Setting Study: A Comparative Review of Nine Prospective Rate-Setting Programs* (Washington, D.C.: Health Care Financing Administration, August 1980).

* REFER TO PG 66

Another key feature of the New Jersey program is its use of interhospital comparisons in setting DRG-specific rates for each hospital. The individual hospital's rate for each DRG is determined by blending statewide standard rates—set separately for major teaching, minor teaching, and nonteaching hospitals—and the individual hospital's actual cost for that DRG. The weight given to the hospital's own cost is directly related to the variation across hospitals in cost for a given DRG.[6]

Massachusetts. The Massachusetts program, signed into law in August 1982, is based on the Blue Cross standard hospital contractual agreement. Each hospital has a maximum allowable cost (MAC) or revenue cap for all payers. Each year's MAC is determined prospectively by rolling forward the hospital's base year costs by the rate of hospital input price inflation, with limited revenue adjustments for increased services. Thus the plan acts like a total revenue constraint with marginal adjustments for volume. The Massachusetts program includes a productivity factor, which assumes that hospitals can increase their operating efficiency. This factor varies from year to year and from payer to payer but averages approximately a 1.25 percent reduction from the MAC. Government payers will have the factor applied first, and it will be phased in later for commercial insurers and Blue Cross; but a downward adjustment of 1.4 percent will be made in the first year to reduce the differential between the payment rates for commercial insurers and Blue Cross. As Massachusetts' hospital costs approach national averages, the productivity increment will be phased out.

Under the Massachusetts system Medicare will pay a share of charity care, but Medicare payments toward bad debt will be limited. Medicare will contribute toward the costs of charity care only in hospitals with a large portion (68 percent or greater) of patients who are on Medicaid or Medicare or who are uninsured. As a condition of the waiver, the secretary of the Department of Health and Human Services required Massachusetts to keep its growth rate in Medicare program costs 1.0 percent below the national average. The program was adopted, given the agreement of Blue Cross and commercial insurers to pay part of the excess if the growth rate in Medicare costs rose above that level.

New York. New York's all-payer plan establishes average per diem rates, adjusted to reflect the ratio of costs to charges for each payer class. The program, effective January 1, 1983, also acts directly as a cap on total hospital revenues since the number of inpatient days in the hospital's base year serves as the target volume for rate setting: only the marginal cost of extra days is paid. Retrospective adjustments for changes in case mix and service are also used.

The new plan holds constant the methodology and base from which hospitals' allowed revenues are rolled forward during the three-year period. This plan reduces the incentives for inflating the hospital's cost base in the short run and, at the same time, enhances the perceived stability and certainty of the rate-setting constraint. The New York program levies a surcharge on all payers to finance regional risk pools designed to offset partially the costs of uncompensated care: charity and bad debt.

Hospital Responses to All-Payer Rate Regulation

The behavioral responses of hospitals to all-payer rate regulation can be classified into the following broad categories:
(HOW TO BEAT SYSTEM)
- cross-subsidization and cost-shift by payer
- changes in volume of inpatient activity
- changes in service intensity and quality
- changes in service mix
- use of medical technology
- vertical and horizontal integration among hospitals and related health care institutions

Cross-Subsidization and Cost-Shift. Some have argued that the advent of Medicare prospective pricing by DRG provides strong impetus for all-payer rate setting. The argument is made that the hospital response to the Medicare system will be to shift unpaid Medicare costs to other payers, particularly to those paying charges.

Although the desire to shift costs may be present, the economic rationale to do so is less clear. Indeed, in the standard economic model, charge-based payers receive price cuts as a result of the Medicare payment charge.[7]

This economic argument views hospitals as profit maximizers with some market power, producing in the declining portion of their long-run cost curves. They charge different prices to different purchasers as a function of the payers' elasticity of demand. Payers with better sources of substitute care pay less. If Medicare pays less as a result of prospective pricing, then hospitals will provide fewer Medicare services. The now-available capacity in the hospital is made available to non-Medicare patients (the next best use of resources). To sell this additional service to the non-Medicare markets, however, prices must be reduced.

73

Recent work in health economics suggests that nonprofit hospitals can be treated analytically as for-profit firms with residual claims accruing to different holders.[8] In such a model profits accruing to voluntary hospitals are used to support activities such as charity care.

In the traditional model profits are reduced; capacity is reallocated across payers; and, if the Medicare price reductions are severe enough, some hospitals close. In the alternative model the same effects are predicted; but, in addition, the uses of profit (charity care, for example), are cut back.

The incentives of a rate-setting program such as that of Medicare do not imply cost-shifting. Rather they imply a scaling back of charity care and perhaps the teaching and research activities of hospitals. The rationale for an all-payer rate-setting program does not stem from cost-shifting. Rather, the justification appears to be all-payer rate-setting as a means of sharing the cost of charity care. The aforementioned experiences in New Jersey and New York seem to support this view.

Volume of Inpatient Activity. The effect of a rate-setting program on hospital volume depends upon the stringency of the regulation and the flexibility that the rate-setting authority allows hospitals. We have argued that hospital volume and services tend to be substitutes.[9] Thus, under programs that set rates per unit of activity (days, cases, services), there is an incentive to substitute around the constraint. The best example is increasing the length of stay under per diem programs, essentially substituting more days of lower average service intensity for fewer days of more intense care.

Evidence from the National Hospital Rate-Setting Study suggests that rate-setting systems have contributed to increased occupancy rates through increased length of stay, rather than through increased admission rates.[10] All three of the programs (New York, New Jersey, and western Pennyslvania) regulating revenues per diem during the study period, 1969–1978, exhibited increased average length of stay. Charge-based programs showed few statistically significant effects, one exception being the finding that lengths of stay and occupancy rates in Maryland hospitals increased. The authors' interpretation was that the incentives of the revenue per unit of service (departmental charge-based structure) regulatory program contributed to this result. In addition, the significant decline in cost per admission in Maryland observed by Coelen and Sullivan [11] may have resulted from a decline in service intensity—principally ancillary service utilization per admission—induced by the incentives of the Maryland

GIR system, which controlled revenues per case for a subset of hospitals.

Nancy Worthington and Paul Piro found little evidence of significant effects of rate-setting on the rate of admissions to hospitals.[12] Thus the volume appears to be dominated by changes in length of stay. These findings may change because New Jersey has moved to per case (diagnosis-adjusted admission) reimbursement for all hospitals and because the number of hospitals covered by Maryland's GIR system has increased since 1978, the end of the period of Worthington and Piro's study.

Service Intensity and Quality. Empirical work concerned with effects of state rate setting on service intensity and quality is limited. Worthington and Piro's findings for New York, New Jersey, and Maryland (the latter two were all-payer systems during the study period) suggest reductions in ancillary service intensity per admission and per patient day. Since reductions in cost per admission were attributed to the regulatory programs in those states, the increased length of stay suggests reduced use of ancillary services.

In a comparison study, David Kidder and Daniel Sullivan found statistically significant reductions in full-time equivalent (FTE) staff per 1,000 adjusted patient days in seven of the twenty-five rate-setting programs.[13] Their results were inconsistent regarding skill mix (which they measured as the share of registered nurses in total employment), but overall they attributed several significant reductions in payroll per adjusted patient day to rate-setting programs.

The observed reductions in service intensity—whether due to increased productivity of labor, reduced ancillary service or capital utilization (all for constant quality), or reduced quality of the process or outcomes of health care—suggest that binding rate regulation does systematically alter the use of hospital input. The key policy question, however, is the degree to which these effects of the rate-setting program are true gains in operating efficiency rather than diminutions in the quality of health care. This important empirical issue is still not settled. Also, the existing data does not permit one to disentangle the effects on service, on intensity, and on quality of all-payer versus non-all-payer programs. Research on this issue has a high priority, and the results of such analyses will influence policy makers' judgments regarding the value of all-payer rate regulation.

Service Mix. Table 4–2 summarizes our estimates of the effect of mandatory state rate-setting programs on the mix of hospital services. The empirical analysis is based on 1980 data on a cross-section of

TABLE 4-2

EFFECT OF MANDATORY STATE RATE-SETTING PROGRAMS ON THE MIX OF HOSPITAL SERVICES, 1980

(statistically significant [p .10] coefficients)

	Services							
	GEN	OPV	PED	SNU	ALLO	OB	ICU	PSY
Per diem[a]								
Massachusetts	(+.09)							
New Jersey non-DRG		(+.09)		(−.07)				
New York			(+.07)	(−.16)				
Total revenue[a]								
Kentucky	(+.08)	(+.03)		(−.09)	(−.04)			
Washington: I	(+.17)			(−.14)				
II	(+.23)			(−.17)	(−.10)			
III	(+.15)			(−.16)				
Wisconsin		(+.03)						
Delaware		(+.03)	(−.02)					
Total revenue[b]								
Colorado		(+.03)			(−.06)			
Connecticut		(+.07)						
Rhode Island		(+.06)						
Vermont		(+.16)						

Per case[a]					
Maryland GIR				(+.03)	
Per case[b]					
New Jersey DRG					
Per unit of service (by department)					
Maryland non-GIR	(+.15)		(−.11)		
Charges					
Indiana	(+.15)				
Missouri		(−.03)	(−.02)		(+.06)
Ohio			(−.08)	(−.01)	(+.03)

NOTES: GEN = general medical-surgical, OPV = outpatient visits, PED = pediatric, SNU = skilled nursing unit, ALLO = all other inpatient, OB = obstetric and gynecologic, ICU = intensive care unit, PSY = psychiatric. The figures presented are proportionate effects of rate-setting programs estimated by the authors.
a. Without adjustment.
b. With adjustment.

MIX =) DEPENDENT VARIABLE

1,502 private, voluntary, not-for-profit hospitals.[14] Eight mutually exclusive and collectively exhaustive categories of hospital services were analyzed: intensive care unit (ICU), pediatric (PED), general medical-surgical (GEN), psychiatric (PSY), obstetric and gynecologic (OB), skilled nursing unit (SNU), outpatient visits (OPV), and all other inpatient services (ALLO). The analysis was directed toward investigating the effect of different types of rate regulation on the proportion of hospital activity in each of the above eight categories. For present purposes, it suffices to emphasize the results for Maryland, New Jersey, and Washington in order to assess all-payer effects in a preliminary fashion, since all three had all-payer programs as of 1980. (Washington's waiver for Medicare and Medicaid ended in 1981.) The coefficients reported in table 4–2 are based on ordinary least squares estimates from a model of the following form:

service mix proportion for type i (i = 1,2,...8) = f (hospital insurance coverage, physician prices, prices of hospital inputs, exogenous market factors shifting the demand for hospital services, hospital-specific teaching status, index of inter-hospital competition in local market area, dummy variables for CON and section 1122 regulations, *plus* a vector of dummy variables to represent particular state rate-setting programs)

This discussion presents the service-mix findings for the three all-payer states as of 1980 using the .10 level of statistical significance as the basis for highlighting significant results. New Jersey's DRG hospitals show no significant (not even marginally) service-mix changes attributable to rate setting. Maryland's non-GIR program, which incorporates a charge-based rate structure based on revenues per unit of service by revenue center, exhibits a pattern similar to New Jersey's non-DRG program: a 15 percent increase in GEN and an 11 percent reduction in SNU relative to hospitals in states without rate setting.[15] The Maryland GIR program results suggest only one significant service-mix adjustment—a 3 percent rise in OB service.

The Washington rate-setting program as of 1980 had three separate components: Type I hospitals were paid based on a percentage of approved budget (modified total revenue program); Type II were paid based on controlled charges subject to a final settlement for volume-adjusted approved revenues; and Type III were paid based on retrospective costs.[16] The Washington findings qualitatively mirror those of the New Jersey and Maryland non-case-mix-based rate-setting programs: increases in GEN and reductions in SNU activity relative to states without rate regulation. Also, in the Type II program a relative decline of 10 percent is observed for the ALLO category.

Accounting profit regressions (American Hospital Association reported revenue minus reported costs) were estimated with a similar model. The results from those estimates may offer a partial explanation for the patterns for the three all-payer programs reported above. Estimates of the incremental (marginal) profit per inpatient day from those regressions [17]—$18.52 per day for GEN (based on a highly statistically significant coefficient) and $4.47 per day for SNU (statistically insignificant)—imply that hospitals under relatively stringent rate-setting programs that cover all payers may shift out of relatively unprofitable and into relatively profitable services. The incentive to engage in profit-enhancing shifts in service mix is increased in a prospective payment regulatory environment, since retrospective cost-based reimbursement in effect taxes away a portion of the hospital's profit. This interpretation is offered only as a plausible conjecture; however, the results are replicated in a longitudinal analysis.

Unlike Conrad and his colleagues, Jerry Cromwell and James Kanak looked at the presence or absence of a selected set of facilities and services.[18] They found that the New Jersey rate-setting program between 1975 and 1978 significantly lowered the rate of adoption of several complex services: ICU, open-heart surgery, burn care, and physical therapy. Interestingly, the Maryland program had no statistically significant effects on complex services attributable to rate-setting during 1976–1978 (which includes the period during which the Medicare and Medicaid waiver was initiated). Washington's program shows only one significant reduction—in the rate of adoption of ICUs in 1978—during its all-payer period. Once again, the evidence is much too limited to estimate the effect on service adoption of the all-payer feature of rate regulation.

Use of Medical Technology. All-payer rate regulation clearly strengthens the incentive to shift sophisticated, expensive technologies out of the regulated hospital setting. Paul Joskow examined the effect of state rate setting on the availability of computerized axial tomographic (CAT) scanning in hospitals.[19] He found that the number of CAT scanners in a state in 1980 was negatively related to the number of years a mandatory rate-setting program had been in effect and that rate setting induced a shift of CAT scanners into physicians' offices.

The general point is that stringent rate regulation is likely to tilt hospitals' decisions regarding the employment of hospital technologies toward those that are cost saving in terms of the specific volume margin (for example, per day or per case) controlled by a given regulatory program. Uses of technology that reduce cost per day, such as through reduced input intensity, may not lead to reductions in cost per case. Furthermore, a population-based approach to evaluating hospital efficiency would require one to examine savings in terms of cost per capita. Technologies that might lower cost per day but increase length of stay or that lower cost per case but involve increased rates of admission or readmission to hospitals, would not necessarily yield long-term savings in total costs per capita. These questions reflect potentially important side effects of rate-setting incentives for policy makers to consider when implementing all-payer (and other) rate regulation programs.

Vertical and Horizontal Integration. All-payer rate regulation creates a market force for increased vertical integration as a means for hospitals to capture the gains from unregulated, nonhospital inpatient services and to enhance the efficiency of their referral relationships with providers. In New Jersey, for example, hospitals have begun operating their own home health agencies and long-term facilities since the implementation of DRG-based reimbursement.[20] This strategy positions the vertically integrated hospital to benefit directly from the reductions in hospital length of stay encouraged by per case payment.

Norms of medical practice permit considerable variation in definitions of the appropriate modes of treatment for a given clinical problem, whereas DRG-based reimbursement promotes more standardized treatment regimens. One way to attenuate this tension between opposing forces on physician treatment choices is to contract directly with physicians and to devise compensation arrangements, such as salaries, which are consistent with reimbursement incentives for hospital behavior. The likelihood that this strategy of hiring one's own medical staff and contracting with primary care physicians in preferred providers to establish referral patterns is enhanced by the increase in the bargaining power of hospital owners and managers vis-à-vis physicians that flows from growth in physician supply relative to patient demand. The vertical integration of medical staff can be viewed as a means for hospitals to induce conformity with behavioral rules that are in the institution's best interest under DRG payment. Clinical standards that place limits on length of stay and on the intensity of preventive, early detection, and diagnostic services are easier to enforce when hospitals have explicit contractual agreements with physicians.

Organizational restructuring of medical and management staff may be necessary to increase physicians' sophistication about the cost consequences of various decisions, to integrate clinical and financial data systems, and to involve physicians at the top management level where long-range capital investment issues concerning the financial feasibility and the clinical efficacy of medical technology are considered.

Rate regulation is also expected to affect the role of physicians in the medical staff of hospitals. Stephen Shortell, Michael Morrisey, and Douglas Conrad argue that rate-setting programs necessitate hospital decisions requiring increased clinical involvement in decision making.[21] Thus they predict more physicians on the hospital board, more physicians in paid administrative positions, and an expanded medical staff committee structure to enhance communication and decision making. They also argue that rate review offers the incentive to integrate administrative and clinical decisions, in part by compensating physicians on salary rather than output-based contracts. Evidence from the 1972–1981 period supports this view but only for the relatively simple changes in medical staff organization. Rate setting apparently has not been onerous enough to necessitate significant organizational change.[22] The work of Bruce Steinwald also supports the increased use of salary compensation of physicians as a result of rate-setting programs.[23]

Finally, if all-payer rate regulation is sufficiently stringent to cause hospitals to sustain continuing operating losses, one can expect a continuation of the current trend toward a more horizontally-integrated hospital sector. Since investor-owned chains tend to avoid the risks to investors inherent in highly regulated markets, increases in the extent of horizontally integrated systems in heavily regulated environments are likely to be concentrated among the nonprofit hospitals. Further, one must be cautious in predicting increased horizontal integration as a behavioral response to all-payer (or generally, more rigorous) rate regulation until much better data are available concerning the mutual operating and financial gains from mergers and other horizontal arrangements. In theory the principal purpose of horizontal agreements in stringently regulated states—for example, all-payer states—would be to improve hospital profit margins through increased operating efficiency. Improved access to the capital markets, one of the documented benefits of multihospital arrangements, is of negligible value unless the financing is backed by a potential for strong operating performance.

Conclusions

This paper, having looked at the likely effects of all-payer rate setting on the operations and organizations of hospitals, comes to six conclusions. First, the form of the program matters. All programs are not equally effective in controlling costs. Underlying this empirical result is that different programs offer different incentives for changing the operations and organization of the hospital.

Second, cost shifting is unlikely to result from the imposition of the Medicare prospective pricing system. The incentives are to cut prices to non-Medicare patients. As a result of Medicare-induced reductions in operating surpluses, hospitals can be expected to reduce their subsidies to nonremunerative services, particularly charity care.

Third, under most forms of rate review the volume of admissions, days, or cases is likely to increase as hospitals cope by adjusting along other paths. The implicit incentive in most programs is to reduce the services contained in the regulated package (that is, in the day, admission, or DRG) and increase the number of packages. Only a total payment limit avoids this incentive.

Fourth, over time services are likely to be eliminated from the hospital. This may result from shifts of potentially free-standing services, such as selected radiologic procedures, to physicians' offices or simply from the elimination of nonremunerative services. Since new technology is likely to be nonremunerative in its early years, the development and diffusion of new medical care products will probably slow.

Fifth, an effective all-payer payment system will necessitate changes in the relations between hospitals and physicians. Physicians will increasingly participate in hospital administrative decisions but will lose a measure of autonomy in treating patients.

Finally, rate-setting programs encourage a search for economies of scale and economies of scope (through the spreading of fixed costs over a broader service mix) to the extent that such economies exist. This reasoning suggests a consolidation of services and continued growth of multihospital systems, albeit with a likely emphasis on nonprofit chains.

Rate-setting programs have pervasive effects on the operations and organization of the hospital and potentially on the health status of the community. Any all-payer rate-setting agency must carefully consider the incentives it wishes to provide.

Notes

1. Karen Cook, Stephen Shortell, Douglas Conrad, et al., "A Theory of Organizational Response to Regulation: The Case of Hospitals," *Academy of Management Review*, vol. 8 (1983), pp. 193–205.

2. Craig Coelen et al., *First Annual Report of the National Hospital Rate-*

Setting Study: A Comparative Review of Nine Prospective Rate-Setting Programs (Washington, D.C.: Health Care Financing Administration, August 1980).

3. Ibid.

4. Ibid.

5. Ibid.

6. Paul L. Grimaldi and Julie A. Micheletti, *Diagnosis-Related Groups: A Practitioner's Guide* (Chicago: Pluribus Press, 1983).

7. J. W. Hay, "The Impact of Public Health Care Financing Policies on Private-Sector Hospital Costs," *Journal of Health Politics, Policy and Law*, vol. 7 (1983), pp. 945–52.

8. Douglas A. Conrad, "Returns on Equity to Not-for-Profit Hospitals: Theory and Implementation," *Health Services Research*, vol. 19 (1984), pp.41–63.

9. M. A. Morrisey, D. A. Conrad, S. M. Shortell, and K. S. Cook, "Hospital Rate Review: A Theory and an Empirical Review," *Journal of Health Economics*, vol. 3 (1984), pp. 25–47.

10. N. L. Worthington and P. A. Piro, "The Effects of Hospital Rate-Setting Programs on Volumes of Hospital Services: A Preliminary Analysis," *Health Care Financing Review*, vol. 4 (1983), pp. 47–66.

11. C. Coelen and D. Sullivan, "An Analysis of the Effects of Prospective Reimbursement Programs on Hospital Expenditures," *Health Care Financing Review*, vol. 2 (1981), pp. 1–40.

12. N. L. Worthington and P. A. Piro, "The Effects of Hospital Rate-Setting Programs on Volumes of Hospital Services: A Preliminary Analysis."

13. David Kidder and Daniel Sullivan, "Hospital Payroll Costs, Productivity, and Employment under Prospective Reimbursement," *Health Care Financing Review*, vol. 4 (1982), pp. 89–100.

14. Douglas A. Conrad, Michael A. Morrisey, Stephen M. Shortell, Karen S. Cook, and Michael K. Chapko, "Economic Regulations and Hospital Behavior: A Theory and Empirical Test for Effects on Service Mix," *Contemporary Policy Issues Series*, forthcoming. An alternative specification of the regulatory variable for the Maryland non-GIR program, in which the proportion of hospital revenues covered by the program is applied as a weight to the dummy variable, gave different results. Under this form there were no statistically significant service-mix effects for Maryland non-GIR. Results for other all-payer programs were not sufficient.

15. Ibid.

16. D. Hamilton, R. Weinstein, A. J. Lee, "Prospective Reimbursement in Washington State," *Topics in Health Care Financing*, vol. 6 (1979), pp. 117–26.

17. Douglas A. Conrad et al., "Economic Regulations and Hospital Behavior."

18. Jerry Cromwell and James Kanak, "An Analysis of the Effects of Prospective Reimbursement Programs on Hospital Adoption and Service Sharing," *Health Care Financing Review*, vol. 2 (1982), pp. 67–88.

19. P. Joskow, *Controlling Hospital Costs: The Role of Government Regulation* (Cambridge, Mass.: MIT Press, 1981).

20. "DRGs Change Hospital Organization, Management," *Medicine and Health Perspectives* (May 30, 1983).

21. S. M. Shortell, M. A. Morrisey, and D. A. Conrad, "Economic Regulation and Hospital Behavior: The Effects on Medical Staff Organization and Hospital–Physician Relationships," *Health Services Research* (in press).

22. Ibid.

23. Bruce Steinwald, "Compensation of Hospital-based Physicans," *Health Services Research*, vol. 18 (1983), pp. 17–43.

5

DRGs and Other Payment Groupings: The Impact on Medical Practice and Technology

Judith L. Wagner

Dramatic changes in the methods that Medicare uses to pay the providers of health care are currently under way or under consideration by Congress. The new Medicare hospital payment system, based on 468 diagnosis-related groups (DRGs), is the most striking example, but changes are in the offing for payment of physicians and other providers as well. Other third-party payers are also altering their traditional approaches to provider payment, both through state-legislated payment systems that cover all payers and through innovative group health plans that encourage efficiency and competition among providers.

These reforms are profoundly different from the cost-containment measures of the 1970s because they are intended to reverse the old financial incentives for providing more and more services rather than counteracting those incentives with regulatory controls. They rest primarily on the concept of *bundling*, the gathering together of services provided as part of an episode or during a period of time. Under the new Medicare system, for example, all services delivered to patients during a hospital stay are bundled into a single rate for each DRG. Prepaid health plans represent the ultimate in bundling of services for payment.

Payment for bundled services cannot exist for long without a way to adjust for differences among patients in their need for services. Otherwise, serious inequities in payment among providers would arise or providers' use of patient selection strategies (that is, cream-

---

This paper is based in part on a study by the Office of Technology Assessment of Diagnosis Related Groups (DRGs) and the Medicare Program. The opinions are those of the author and do not express those of OTA or its board.

skimming) would be encouraged for classifying episodes of illness or patients according to the relative costs of providing care efficiently. The DRG patient classification system, with its 468 categories, is the backbone of bundled per-case hospital payment.

If bundled payment is successful, in the coming years we should expect to see a relative slowdown in the flow of funds into the health care sector. The new incentives have implications for the efficiency and quality of care delivered to Medicare and other patients and for the settings in which medical technologies are used. Will these changes be beneficial for patients? Perhaps even more important, new methods of payment will affect technological change in medicine, causing the adoption of new technologies and the elimination of old ones. Technological change should act as a filtering process, continually winnowing out the less useful in favor of the more useful technologies. To what extent can the new payment methods be expected to improve or hinder this process? Finally, to what extent can payment systems based on bundles of services stay abreast of and encourage appropriate technological change?

This paper attempts to address these questions. The first section focuses on the Medicare DRG payment system and explores the implications of that system for the use of technology and for technical change. Particular emphasis is placed on the implications of the still-to-be-developed process for adjusting DRG prices over time. The second section looks at some other kinds of cost-containment strategies, particularly in the physician payment area, that could affect the use of medical technology.

DRG Hospital Payment and Medical Technology

In April 1983 the president signed into law a sweeping revision of Medicare's inpatient hospital payment system (P.L. 98–21).[1] Begun in October 1983, the new payment method will evolve over a three-year transition period into a national set of per-case prices for treating patients with specific diagnostic and therapeutic characteristics.

Despite the speed with which DRG payment was enacted into law, no empirical evidence is available on the effect per-case payment in general, or DRG payment in particular, has on the use of or the access to medical technologies. There has been only limited experience in the states. New Jersey has, since 1978, implemented an all-payer per-case payment system using DRGs, and Maryland has made a case-mix adjustment to its per-admission rates. The effects of these somewhat different systems on the use of services within or outside hospitals, however, are not yet known.

Evidence is available from other types of hospital prospective payment schemes (that is, programs in which rates are set before the period during which they apply and in which the hospital is at some financial risk). For example, programs that pay hospitals by the day increase the average length of stay and occupancy rates relative to cost-based payment.[2] Studies of the impact of hospital rate setting on the adoption of new medical technologies by hospitals have found some effects, but much depends on the strength and design of the program.[3] New York State's per-day payment system, the oldest and most restrictive hospital rate-setting program, has clearly altered the extent and availability of new technology in hospitals.

Taken as a whole, the results above suggest that decision makers in hospitals respond in predictable ways to financial incentives for the adoption and use of hospital technologies. Consequently, in the absence of empirical evidence on the effects of DRG payment on the adoption and use of medical technology, an assessment of the direction and strength of the financial incentives of that type of payment is reasonable.

Under DRG payment there exist two fundamental incentives that ultimately translate into specific demands for medical technologies. These incentives are to reduce the cost to the hospital of each inpatient hospital stay and to increase the number of inpatient admissions.

Reducing cost per case is the motivation for per-case payment in the first place. Per-case payment is predicated on the belief that hospitals have many opportunities to save money by operating more efficiently and offering a more cost-effective mix of services. Per-case payment rewards hospitals that take advantage of these opportunities. Reductions in the cost per admission can be achieved by reducing the length of stay (LOS), the number or mix of services provided during the stay, or the prices paid for inputs into the production of hospital services. Reductions in LOS are likely to have the greatest immediate effects on per-case costs (although such savings would be lower for hospitals already operating at low occupancy rates). Recent studies have demonstrated that the well-known regional differences in average LOS in the United States persist even when the diagnosis and the severity of illness are taken into account.[4] Thus there may be substantial room for reduction of LOS in some areas of the country.

The incentives inherent in DRG payment regarding the use of particular ancillary technologies are complex. The cost of ancillary services, the use of which would on the average shorten hospital LOS, would be weighed against the savings from reductions in LOS. The effect on any particular ancillary technology would depend on the nature of these cost tradeoffs. For example, a hospital might provide more high-cost antibiotics prophylactically if these were shown to reduce the average LOS substantially through reductions in hospital-acquired infection rates. As another example, liaison psychiatric services, which have been shown to shorten LOS in postoperative elderly patients,[5] might be provided more frequently under DRG payment than under cost-based reimbursement. Nevertheless, if the consensus is correct that ancillary services, particularly diagnostic tests, have been provided in the past without adequate consideration for their effect on total hospital costs,[6] then the net effect of per-case payment will be to reduce the intensity or the amount of these services per stay.

There is an obvious incentive to reduce the price of technologies such as drugs and medical supplies. In the past ten years, hospitals have increasingly embraced membership in group purchasing-plans and generic-drug substitution programs. Hospital membership in pharmaceutical-purchasing groups grew from 40 percent to 88 percent between 1975 and 1981.[7] Generic substitution—the automatic substitution of a less costly but chemically equivalent generic drug for a prescribed brand-name drug—has become commonplace in U.S. hospitals: 96 percent of hospitals responding to a national survey in 1981 reported having such programs.[8] The pressure to find new ways to save on the purchase of drugs and supplies should continue. A logical outcome of this trend would be a decline in product variation as hospitals and their purchasing groups seek further price reductions and strengthen the competitive position of those manufacturers with high sales volumes.

The incentive to increase admissions operates selectively. Whereas cost- and charge-based reimbursement gave hospitals an incentive to keep occupancy rates high by increasing either admissions or LOS, under DRG payment only admissions produce or increase revenues. Every new admission generates new revenues (in the amount of the DRG price) and new costs. Serving patients in some DRGs will be more profitable than in others, and hospitals will naturally want to encourage the more profitable admissions. If the average level of payment is high enough that all DRGs are profitable, then hospitals will have an incentive to increase admissions in general; but the most profitable admissions would still be sought more vigorously. Also, since much diversity exists among patients within particular DRGs, hospitals may have opportunities to be selective in admitting less severely ill patients.

Various mechanisms are available to increase admissions selectively, such as recruiting physicians in key specialties, adopting services useful in certain profitable DRGs, and targeting marketing campaigns to preferred patients or their physicians.

Competition for patients is likely to influence the specialization of services, but the direction of these effects will probably vary across DRG categories. On the one hand, competition can stimulate specialization of services.[9] Since the per-unit costs of major services often decline as service volumes increase, hospitals with high service volumes in specific DRGs will find them more profitable, and those with low volumes less so. When a hospital finds that a service is unprofitable and when the prospects for more efficient operation or increases in volume are dim, it may cut its losses by abandoning the service. For example, a hospital in New Jersey recently closed its hyperbaric chamber because it was found to be unprofitable under the state's DRG payment system.[10] On the other hand, competition for admissions can drive hospitals to maintain unprofitable services if their continued existence is important to the long-run survival of the hospital.

When combined, the reduction of cost per case and the increase in admissions encourage the development of services at alternative sites, particularly those not subject to bundled payment. Indeed, the hallmark of bundled payment is that it establishes incentives to unbundle services, that is, to provide services in settings or environments where additional payment can be expected. Widespread adoption of preadmission outpatient testing can be expected, of course. The incentive to discharge patients early will also encourage the use of nursing homes and home health services, which at present are reimbursed by Medicare on a reasonable cost basis.[11] The lack of an "outlier" policy with respect to low-cost admissions, however, will encourage hospitalization for patients with conditions that might have been diagnosed or treated on an outpatient basis. (This incentive will, of course, necessitate active monitoring and review of admissions patterns, thus requiring once again regulatory oversight for the purposes of cost control.)

The incentives under DRG pricing are also likely to affect the introduction of new technologies in the hospital. Many observers have predicted that per-case payment creates incentives for hospitals to adopt new cost-saving technologies. Yet, because technologies are neither cost-saving nor cost-raising independent of the context in which they are used, all hospitals cannot be expected to adopt the same technologies. The introduction of new capital-intensive cost-saving technologies under DRG payment will probably enhance the process of specialization as small hospitals become unable to reap the cost-saving benefits of some investments. Some technologies that depend on high volume to be cost-saving could be provided to smaller hospitals on a contract basis by large hospitals or independent laboratories. The feasibility of such arrangements would vary with the specific uses of a technology and the geographical and competitive environment in which the hospitals operate.

The introduction of new cost-raising technology—that which raises the hospital's per-case cost—is discouraged but not eliminated under DRG payment. Unlike cost-based payment, DRG payment does not meet new costs with a concomitant increase in revenues. New technology must compete with alternative uses of funds, such as employee wage and benefit increases or additional nursing staff. New technology may be at an additional disadvantage compared with other uses of funds because of the relative uncertainty about its benefits in the early stages of diffusion.[12] Thus, with limited resources, hospitals will need to assess new technologies more closely and ration resources more carefully.

Nevertheless, some new cost-raising technologies may actually be introduced more swiftly and widely under DRG payment because of their potential effect on the competitive position of the hospital. Despite its high capital and operating costs, for example, nuclear magnetic resonance (NMR) imaging may be highly desirable to hospitals seeking to protect their admissions base from encroachment by other hospitals. Thus, although DRG payment implies that in general new technologies will be adopted less swiftly and widely than under cost-based reimbursement, highly visible individual exceptions will persist, and technological change is unlikely to approach a standstill.

DRG Price Adjustments and Medical Technology

If DRG payment is to continue to function effectively, adjustments to the price structure will be necessary. The long-run viability of the DRG payment system depends on its ability both to adapt to appropriate technological change and to encourage it in medicine. If the payment system remains rigid in the face of medical progress, it will become unacceptable to providers, patients, and the public. Consequently, the DRG payment system must encompass procedures for timely adjustment to new economic and technological conditions as they arise.

Much attention is now being devoted to the issue of how DRG prices should change with the passage of time. The new Medicare law requires annual adjustments in the average DRG payment rate to account for inflation and technological change; it also requires recalibration of DRG prices relative to one another at least once every four years.

Only changes in the absolute or average price level can increase the revenue flowing to hospitals; any increase in the relative price of one DRG implies corresponding decreases in the actual prices received for all other DRGs.

The newly created Prospective Payment Assessment Commission (PROPAC) is charged with recommending to the secretary of the Department of Health and Human Services (DHHS) both an annual absolute price adjustment and the needs for updating relative DRG prices. Since the law specifies that relative prices must be recalculated at least every four years, both DHHS and PROPAC must concern themselves with these issues at least that often. The annual average price must reflect technological change as well as the effects of general price inflation, but the amount of the increase is not statutorily specified. The changes in relative DRG prices are required to reflect "changes in treatment patterns, technology, and other factors which may change the relative use of hospital resources."[13] Beyond these general requirements, however, the law is silent; and, because the first recalibration must occur by October 1985, active discussion is now under way both in DHHS and PROPAC about the implications of various approaches to DRG price adjustments for hospitals or technologies.

The primary objectives of a DRG price adjustment are three-fold: (1) to provide an adequate level of resources to fund the continued operation of the hospital system; (2) to maintain equality across DRGs (and the patients they represent) in the ratios of DRG price to the cost of providing care efficiently; and (3) to provide adequate incentives for hospitals to introduce new technologies that, although cost-raising to the hospital, are worth their costs to society. The first objective could be met by generous increases in the absolute DRG price level. The second objective is more difficult to meet. As the cost of efficient care in each DRG changes over time, so, too, should the relative DRG price. If it were reasonable to expect that costs would increase or decrease uniformly across all DRGs, then the only problem would be to select annually an average DRG update rate. But uniform cost increases are highly unlikely. Some DRGs will experience cost-saving changes, while others will be subject to cost increases. The relative prices of inputs (such as personnel, supplies, and energy) will also have an effect on relative DRG costs. In the absence of any changes in relative DRG prices, the ratio of DRG price to efficient cost would show increasing divergence across DRG categories. As these ratios diverge, certain DRGs would become generally more profitable, others less so, and hospitals would have greater incentives to engage in selective admitting strategies, possibly leaving some patients with inadequate access to care.

91

The simplest method for keeping relative prices in line with costs is periodically to reestimate relative DRG costs using the methods and data bases that were used by the Health Care Financing Administration (HCFA) to establish the initial set of relative rates. Although periodic reestimation represents an attempt to measure historical costs, not the costs of providing care by the most efficient method possible, the new competitive discipline imposed by DRG payment ensures that, as time passes, actual costs will approach efficient costs. Reestimation would, of course, necessitate the ongoing and timely availability of both the Medicare cost reports and patient claims data that show charges by department. Although this availability is politically unpalatable, the hospital industry should be aware of the implications of not having such data available: the eventual disassociation of prices from costs and a breakdown of the DRG payment system.

The third objective, not to discourage the adoption of beneficial technologies even though they are cost-raising, presents a particular challenge to the DRG adjustment system. It entails making one-time adjustments in relative DRG rates or in the structure of DRGs themselves to accommodate new technology. Two general methods of relative DRG price adjustment can be used for inducing desirable technological change: unconditional and conditional adjustments. Unconditional adjustments in relative DRG rates would apply to all hospitals (or to an entire class of hospitals) whether or not they adopt or use a new technology. Conditional relative DRG price adjustments are those granted to hospitals only if they actually adopt or use the technology. The unconditional adjustment methods are the following:

• *Periodic empirical reestimation of relative DRG costs.* It is feasible to rely on statistical reestimation to reflect new cost structures imposed by new medical technologies. The method is reactive: as technological change alters the costs of serving patients in specific DRGs, the calculated rates change. The process is also gradual, since estimated relative costs would be based on a blend of costs experienced by both adopters and nonadopters of new technology. Only in the final stages of diffusion, when a technology is uniformly applied across all hospitals and all patients in a given class, would the estimated relative costs reflect the full cost increase.

• *Central policy decision to change relative DRG rates.* DHHS could make purposeful adjustments in relative DRG prices to reflect changes in economic or technological conditions. An increase in the rate paid for a particular DRG relative to all others could be used as a means of funding the acquisition of a cost-raising technology. Of course, hospitals treating patients in the DRG with the increased rate would be free to use the new revenue for any purpose.

Conditional adjustments in relative DRG prices could be accomplished in two ways:

• *Creation of new DRGs.* New DRGs, differentiated from preexisting ones by the use of a specific technology, can be created as a way of paying a hospital only if it actually adopts and uses a technology. The new DRG would be assigned a price reflecting the higher or lower resource costs associated with the use of the new technology. For example, liver transplantation might become its own DRG, with a price granted to any hospital performing that procedure.

• *Provider-initiated appeals.* Although the new Medicare law specifically prohibits hospitals from appealing DRG rates, this approach is potentially useful for case-by-case exceptions to DRG prices to pay for new cost-raising technology. (It is safe to presume that hospitals would not request rate reductions due to cost-saving innovations.) The Medicare law does allow appeals for very high cost outlier patients on a case-by-case basis, a mechanism that could indirectly be used to finance some new technologies.

The unconditional price adjustment methods are not completely satisfactory for bringing about desirable cost-raising technological change. Periodic reestimation of DRG costs is not likely to be sufficient to induce hospitals to adopt all desirable cost-increasing technology, especially technologies that are very expensive to the hospital. Early adopters would bear the full extra costs of such new technology, but the updated weights based on averaging costs across both adopters and nonadopters would not reflect the full increase in per-case costs. Hence, the initial stages of the diffusion process would be underfinanced. (This does not imply, however, that hospitals would never adopt cost-raising technologies. Some would undoubtedly see the benefits of early adoption of useful new technologies, particularly visible ones, and would make the investment.) With central policy decisions to change relative DRG rates, the hospital would be free to use the extra payment for any purpose. Thus these across-the-board adjustments would give equal reward to both adopters and nonadopters.

Yet conditional adjustment mechanisms, such as the creation of new DRGs or individual provider appeals, have their own shortcomings. Creation of new DRGs may appear on the surface to be an ideal approach, but it has serious deficiencies as a long-run adjustment mechanism. The prospect of "DRG inflation"—the gradual increase in the number of categories—would soon render hospital billing forms unwieldy and would make management of data all the more difficult. If the experience with medical procedure nomenclature is any guide, the rate of increase in the number of categories can be expected to be high.[14] The first revision in DRG nomenclature increased the number of categories by 22 percent. More important, over time DRG payment would come to look more and more like fee-for-service medicine, in which the amount of payment is inextricably linked to the procedures performed. Financial incentives to perform profitable combinations of procedures could reappear. In addition, the substitution of new cost-saving procedures for more expensive ones would be discouraged if patients were bumped out of higher-priced DRGs into lower-priced ones as a result. Thus the uncontrolled expansion of categories can ultimately create a more rigid, less cost-effective health care delivery system.

Extensive reliance on case-by-case hospital appeals of DRG rates is not only administratively costly and cumbersome, but it, too, ultimately leads to a fee-for-service system in which a hospital can receive more if it does more. Thus conditional adjustment approaches apparently must be applied with the utmost restraint and only in cases in which other adjustment techniques are clearly inadequate.

What do all of these considerations mean for a DRG adjustment process? In general, they imply that adequate concern for an absolute rate of payment that generates sufficient surplus to invest in appropriate new technology, combined with frequent, even annual, reestimation of relative costs, should be the main vehicle for dealing with cost-raising technological change. Tampering with relative prices using either conditional or unconditional approaches should be reserved for the very few high-cost technologies the adoption of which would be prohibitively expensive without an adjustment. Then the decision would have to be made whether the best approach would be (1) to make an across-the-board change in a relative DRG price; (2) to create one or more new DRGs; or (3) to resort to case-by-case appeals. The best approach would seem to depend upon the specific medical and economic characteristics of the new technology. If a technology is expected to diffuse widely and uniformly through all patients within a DRG, for example, across-the-board adjustment in the relative price of that DRG would be the best approach. Conversely, if the technology is best limited to specific hospitals or medical teams with special skills, the case-by-case appeals would be the appropriate mechanism.

Extending DRGs to Physician Payment: Implications for Technology

Clearly, the DRGs as developed do not adequately represent physicians' case mix, but the possibility of developing patient-based categories for payment of physicians has received much support, and research is currently underway in several institutions to create ambulatory care classification systems analogous to the DRG system. Payment by episode of illness or by severity-adjusted visit is the ultimate goal of those who would extend the per-case payment philosophy to physician payment. The first application of the principle would be likely to involve physicians' care to hospitalized patients, particularly to surgical patients.

The question is how such a change, occurring in conjunction with DRG payment of hospitals, would likely affect the ways in which medical technologies are adopted and used. Here again, there is virtually no empirical evidence on which to draw for predictions. Though some would claim that the experience of prepaid health plans is indicative of the effects of bundling services for the purposes of payment, it is questionable whether the historical experience with these providers is relevant to imposing a Medicare-wide payment system. Moreover, a per-episode or per-visit payment is inherently different from payment on a per-capita basis and would lead to different patterns of technology use.

Just as per-case payment sets up basic incentives, so, too, does per-episode payment of physicians. In this case, the financial incentives would be to provide as few services as possible per episode and to maximize the number of separate episodes of care. Thus paying physicians a fixed amount for services to hospitalized patients would probably lead to fewer visits and fewer or more consultations (depending on whether these services were included in the flat rate), with fewer tests ordered as a consequence of such visits. Certain physician-performed tests, such as sigmoidoscopy, could well decline in their rate of use if they could no longer be separately billed. Such incentives would reinforce those inherent in DRG payment of hospitals and therefore might seriously weaken one of the best safeguards against underprovision of care in the current DRG payment system: the power and willingness of the physician to act as the patient's advocate.

Per-episode rates applied to ambulatory care would also reward increases in the number of separate episodes and reductions in the number of the services rendered per episode. The principal outcome of such a payment system would probably be a dramatic reduction in the amount of ambulatory laboratory testing. Recent studies suggest that tests performed in the physician's office are lucrative. To the extent that the financial incentives created by present methods of payment have increased the rate of testing in physicians' offices, per-episode payment would have the reverse effect.

As an add-on to DRG payment of hospitals, per-episode payment for ambulatory care could either reinforce or counteract the incentive to increase hospital admissions. The net effect would depend upon the relative payment rates for hospital-based episodes and office-based episodes in relation to the cost of providing such care. If, for example, the return on the physician's time associated with visiting a hospitalized patient were still higher than the return on office-based episodes of illness, the physician's incentives to hospitalize the patient would actually increase. Thus the structure of relative prices under an ambulatory per-episode payment system might have an even stronger influence on the use of technology and the cost of healthcare than does the structure of relative prices in DRG hospital payment. Per-episode relative prices would require the same kinds of adjustment for new technologies that DRG relative prices do. Fiberoptic endoscopy procedures, for example, have been estimated to cost office-based physicians between $30 and $90 when performed at the rate of fifteen per week.[15] (Undoubtedly, the procedure was more expensive when first applied by a few physicians.) What physician would have been willing to perform this procedure as part of an illness episode paid at a total rate of $100 or even $150? Even when performed in the hospital, using equipment and personnel supplied by the hospital, the procedure is time-intensive for the physician. One can conjecture on the speed with which fiberoptic endoscopy would have been introduced in such an inhospitable payment environment. Any per-episode pricing system would inevitably be forced to deal with technological issues such as that posed by endoscopy.

Conclusions

The increasing trend away from fee-for-service payment and toward payment for bundles of service is likely to have major effects on the way that medical technology is adopted and used in the practice of medicine. In general, these effects will depend upon the definition of the unit of payment around which services are bundled. A strong case can certainly be made for the broadest possible unit of payment, even one that combines all covered services. Broader definitions encourage substitution among alternative inputs in the most efficient manner and discourage attempts to move patients from bundled settings into those settings still paid for on a fee-for-service basis. They also make it harder for providers to increase the number of units of services provided as a way of generating revenue.

Bundling also has a cost, however. There is always the fear that the incentive to provide each unit of service at the least possible cost will be abused, with negative consequences for patients' health. In the case of hospital DRG prices, that physicians continue to be paid on a fee-for-service basis and therefore do not have the same incentives as the hospital administrator is reassuring. Inclusion of the physician in the per-case payment would eliminate that safeguard.

Perhaps more important, bundling of services for payment requires constant attention to the structure of relative prices. The more bundled the system is, the more difficult it becomes to keep relative.

Notes

1. This section draws on a technical memorandum by the Office of Technology Assessment entitled, *Diagnosis Related Groups (DRGs) and the Medicare Program: Implications for Medical Technology* (July 1983).

2. N. Worthington and P. Piro, "The Effects of Hospitals' Rate Setting Programs on Volumes of Hospital Services," *Health Care Financial Review*, vol. 4, no. 2 (1982), p. 47.

3. J. Cromwell and J. Kanak, "The Effects of Prospective Reimbursement Programs on Hospital Adoption and Service Sharing," *Health Care Financing Review*, vol. 4, no. 2 (December 1982), p. 67; P. Joskow, *Controlling Hospital Costs: The Role of Government Regulation* (Cambridge, Mass: MIT Press, 1981); J. Wagner, M. Krieger, R. Lee, et al., "A Study of the Impact of Reimbursement Strategies on the Diffusion of Medical Technologies, Vol. 1. Summary and Findings," Final Report of Grant from Health Care Financing Administration (Grant No. 18-P-97113) (Washington, D.C.: The Urban Institute, 1982).

4. M. C. Hornbrook, "HCUP Research Note 3: Regional Differences in Length of Hospital Stay," National Center for Health Services Research, 1983; U.S. Congress, Office of Technology Assessment, "Variations in Hospital Length of Stay: Their Relationship to Health Outcomes," background paper prepared by M. Chassin (contract no. 233-7210.0), 1983.

5. S. Levitan, and D. Kornfeld, "Clinical and Cost Benefits of Liaison Psychiatry," *American Journal of Psychiatry*, vol. 138, no. 6 (1981), p. 790.

6. H. L. Abrams, "The Overutilization of X-Rays," *New England Journal of Medicine*, vol. 300 (1979), p. 12313; P. Griner and R. Glaser, "Misuse of Laboratory Tests and Diagnostic Procedures," *New England Journal of Medicine*, vol. 307, no. 21 (1982), pp. 1336–39; T. Maloney and D. Rogers, "Medical

Technology—A Different View of the Contentious Debate over Costs," *New England Journal of Medicine*, vol. 301, no. 26 (1979), pp. 1413–45; L. Myers and S. Schroeder, "Physician Use of Services for the Hospitalized Patient: A Review, with Implications for Cost Containment," *Milbank Memorial Fund Quarterly*, vol. 59 (1981), pp. 481–507.

7. Eli Lilly & Co., *Lilly Hospital Pharmacy Survey '82* (1982); M. H. Stolar, "National Survey of Selected Hospital Pharmacy Practices," *American Journal of Hospital Pharmacy*, vol. 33 (1976), pp. 225–30.

8. M. H. Stolar, ibid.

9. S. E. Berki, "The Design of Case-Based Hospital Payment Systems," *Medical Care*, vol. 21, no. 1 (1983), p. i.

10. New Jersey Department of Health and HSA, Regional Health Planning Council, Application Abstract and Record, State Application No. 821108-07-01, HSA Application No. 82-101 (December 1982).

11. Though reimbursement is subject to limits, they are not as rigid as DRG payment. For example, reimbursement for home health care services are subject to a per-visit limit, but all ancillary services delivered as part of the visit are reimbursed on a cost basis.

12. A. A. Romeo, J. Wagner, and R. Lee, "Prospective Hospital Reimbursement and the Diffusion of New Hospital Technologies," *Journal of Health Economics*, vol. 3 (1984), pp. 1–24.

13. U.S. Congress, H.R. Report 98-47, p. 98.

14. J. Mitchell and J. Cromwell, "Alternative Methods for Describing Physician Services Performed and Billed," prepared for the Health Care Financing Administration, Contract No. 500-81-0054 (October 12, 1982).

15. J. Showstack and S. Shroeder, *The Cost and Effectiveness of Upper Gastrointestinal Endoscopy*, U.S. Congress Office of Technology Assessment, Case Study (1981); B. F. Overholt, "The Costs of Endoscopy and Alternatives: The Current State of Knowledge," presented at the National Institutes of Health Consensus Development Conference on Endoscopy in Upper GI Bleeding, Bethesda, Md., August 20–22, 1980.

6

Physicians and Hospitals: Changing Dynamics

Ruth S. Hanft

Historians will view the 1980s as a watershed era in the history of American medicine because major, rapid changes are affecting all aspects of the health sector. The last great revolution, the Flexnerian reform of medical education, changed the scientific basis of physicians' practice and stimulated rapid technological advances that set the pattern for health care for seventy years. In the early 1900s, Dr. Abraham Flexner was commissioned by the American Medical Association and the Carnegie Foundation to review the state of American medical education. There had been a rapid growth of proprietary medical schools with few standards for admission or qualifications for graduation. The reform of medical education and technological advances spurred by this reform dramatically affected physicians' ability to intervene in illness and their roles, practice patterns, power, and autonomy in society. Hospitals, which had been warehouses for the dying and the poor, became laboratories for a new type of physician.

The growing recognition of the value of physicians' skills during the past seven decades has made the physician the focal point for decisions about most aspects and sites of health care.[1] The physician became the key determinant of demand for services and consequently for expenditures. This central role was enhanced by the development of third-party payments that reduced the cost of care at the time of service and ensured payment to the physician for most of the care decisions. Policies of third-party payers recognized virtually all costs, particularly for services provided in hospitals, and for most tests and procedures.

The methods of payment, retroactive reasonable costs for hospitals and fee-for-service payments to physicians, by their very nature stimulated increases in the volume and intensity of service and expansion of capital and technology. Physicians incurred few costs for treatment decisions, and hence they had no incentive to withhold even marginally useful diagnosis or treatment modalities. Furthermore, when physicians practiced in the hospital, they bore none of the costs of the facility, equipment, or hospital staff. Until recently, the hospital had no incentive to constrain these decisions. In addition, consumers, inhibited by lack of technical knowledge and protected from financial consideration by health insurance, also had little direct economic stake.[2]

Three factors are rapidly changing this oversimplified description of twentieth-century American health care. These factors will have profound effects on the dynamics among consumers, physicians, and hospitals. At one extreme these factors will cause increased conflict among the parties; at the other extreme they may spur new symbiotic relationships between physicians and hospitals. The consumer, depending on financial incentives and increased information, probably will play a larger role in the redistribution of resources among hospitals and physicians and in the total demand for services. The four factors that will have a powerful effect on physician/hospital relations are

- the dramatic increase in physician supply
- changes in hospital reimbursement and in physician payment during the next several years
- stimulation of competition and the entry of venture capital into the health field
- the corporatization of American medicine—profit and nonprofit

Increased Supply of Physicians

The anticipation of the passage of Medicare and its subsequent enactment stimulated public policy concerns and discussion that there would be an inadequate supply of physicians to meet new demands for care. The number of medical schools and the physician-to-population ratios had declined precipitously after the Flexner report. Furthermore, as demand for medical services increased with the advent of health insurance, physician growth lagged. Physicians were deserting small towns, rural areas, and inner cities. In the 1950s, foreign medical graduates were given immigration priorities to help fill the gap. The American Medical Association fought direct federal funding of medical education until the 1960s. In the 1960s and 1970s, the federal government began to support medical education directly to encourage expansion in the number of schools and in enrollment levels in existing schools, first through construction and institutional grants and then through capitation and bonuses for increased enroll-ment.[3] States expanded the schools within their state university systems and added new schools. By 1980 the number of medical schools had grown from 80 to 127, and enrollment had doubled. Osteopathic schools grew from six to fifteen.

Medical education is a long process, seven years at the minimum (five years for osteopathic medicine) from entry into medical school to practice. Although the Graduate Medical Education National Advisory Committee Report of 1980 (GMENAC) signaled concern about an emerging oversupply of physicians,[4] enrollment growth continued until 1982–1983.[5] Furthermore, an estimated 3,000–4,000 U.S. citizens are studying abroad each year. The increased supply will not peak until well into the 1990s, but some of the effects are already beginning to be observed. For example, physicians are establishing practices in small towns; geographic distribution has improved, and there has been a decline in the number of underserved areas.[6]

Today it has become increasingly difficult for physicians to establish private practices in certain urban areas like Boston and Washington. It has also become more difficult financially to establish a solo practice or to find a partnership with an active group of physicians in a desirable area. One result has been that more physicians are willing to accept salaried job contracts and work for health maintenance organizations (HMOs) and hospitals.

The rate of increase in physicians' income has slowed. In 1984 that rate rose at a level below the general inflation rate. For some types of physicians net income declined. Physicians are beginning to extend office hours and make house calls,[7] work in more than one site, and advertise their services.

The authors of the GMENAC report, economists, and public policy experts have been concerned that the ability of physicians to generate demand for services, in concert with the increased supply of physicians, will have further inflationary effects on health care costs and expenditures. Changes in reimbursement and the effects of competition, however, may modify the ability of physicians to generate demand and increase expenditures.

Changes in Hospital Reimbursement and Potential Changes in Payments for Physicians' Services

Hospitals. Before the passage of Medicare in 1965, hospitals were paid through several different arrangements: costs with discounts, costs plus a factor for capital expansion, charges, negotiated rates, and philanthropic contributions.[8] Radiology, pathology, and anesthesiology were largely hospital-based services, and many physicians in these specialties were salaried at the hospital. Unlike other specialties, there was usually no separation of payment to the hospital and the physician for these services.

When Medicare was enacted, the decision was made to pay hospitals on a retroactive reasonable cost basis and to pay separately for physicians' services in anesthesiology, radiology, and pathology as well as for other specialties. The consequences of relatively open-ended cost reimbursement, whatever the expenditure, produced incentives to provide more services and add equipment and personnel, since virtually all costs were covered.[9]

These incentives became apparent soon after the enactment of Medicare. Over time, numerous efforts were made to reverse this trend and to contain inflation in hospital costs caused by the Medicare payment method. These efforts included the imposition of limits on routine hospital costs;[10] the economic stabilization program of the Nixon and Ford eras; and, in 1982, limits on ancillary costs.[11] None of these efforts, however, were directed specifically toward influencing physician behavior, the key to controlling health care utilization.

Major revisions in Medicare reimbursement were enacted in the 1982 Tax Equity and Fiscal Responsibility Act and the 1983 Social Security amendments. These legislative changes radically altered the basis for payments to hospitals and all of the prior incentives in hospital reimbursement. The new per-case method of payment will be phased in over a period of four years, and at the end of the period all acute care general hospitals will be paid on the basis of national average rates for 468 diagnosis related groups (DRGs). Hospitals that have costs exceeding these rates will lose revenue; hospitals that have costs below these rates will profit.

Several criticisms about the new method of payment have been voiced. One is that DRGs do not measure differences in the severity of illness within the diagnosis.[12] Within the same diagnosis, patients can have varying degrees of intensity of illness. DRGs also may overprice some diagnoses and underprice others.

The new pricing system has already affected the dynamics between physicians and hospital administrators.[13] In the past, physicians had almost unlimited decision-making power (except for utilization review) on admissions, lengths of stay, and selection of ancillary services. Under the new reimbursement, patterns of physicians' practice that raise costs above the average will have to be reviewed if hospitals are to remain fiscally viable. Hospitals have already implemented data analysis systems to compare physicians' practice patterns and to alert the hospital administrator or its medical director to practice patterns that exceed payment limits. Physicians may find their hospital privileges restricted or withdrawn if they consistently exceed the limits.

The incentives in DRG reimbursement are designed to shorten, and have already shortened, lengths of stay, since total payment remains the same whether the patient stays two or ten days. To shorten lengths of stay, hospitals will try, whenever possible, to substitute lower-cost services, such as the use of extended-care facilities and home health agencies. The incentives are also to substitute out-of-hospital services that are not controlled by the DRG payment system, such as preadmission diagnostic tests and day surgery. Furthermore, since the payment is set by diagnosis rather than by service, the incentive is to reduce the number of services per case. Finally, since DRGs do not distinguish severity of illness within the diagnosis, there is an incentive to treat less ill patients and refer the severely ill to other institutions.

The DRG reimbursement method not only encourages hospital intervention in physician practice, it also sets up a competitive environment among hospitals and among physicians, hospitals, and corporations for control of certain services, particularly profitable services and sites of services that are not covered by prospective payment.[14] Today we are witnessing explosive growth in the number of physicians, corporations, and hospitals sponsoring free-standing surgicenters, diagnostic centers, HMOs, wellness and fitness centers, and home health agencies. To date, no reimbursement controls have been placed on health care delivery organizations and sites other than hospitals, nursing homes, hospices, and renal dialysis centers.

Changes in hospital payment are also occurring in the private sector and in state Medicaid programs. Preferred provider organizations (PPOs), stimulated by employers and insurance companies, are negotiating discounted prices with hospitals and are seeking bids from hospitals to care for their enrollees. Similarly, states are negotiating fixed prices and seeking low-cost hospitals for Medicaid patients.

Physicians. Changes in payment to physicians have begun, and further changes are anticipated. HMOs provide physician and hospital services on the basis of a per capita payment (capitation). As HMOs continue to grow and develop, capitation payments and salaried practices will become increasingly common. Since HMOs provide the full range of inpatient and outpatient services and physicians' remuneration is dependent on the balance between the use of inpatient and outpatient care, the incentives for physicians practicing in HMOs are to reduce hospitalization. Furthermore, capitation payments stimulate substitution of lower-skilled nonphysician personnel where possible and promote tight control of ancillary services and referrals so that the HMO and physicians can retain a larger share of the capitated fees that the HMO receives.

When Congress enacted the Medicare prospective hospital payment provision, it included as a requirement that the Health Care Financing Administration (HCFA) report by January 1986 the feasibility of DRG physician payment. Although this approach may not be feasible for all physician services, it may be a feasible strategy to pay for surgery and in-hospital medical care. Discussions are also being held about the possibility of substituting fee schedules for payment of usual, customary, and reasonable charges. As a first step toward altering physician payment, the Deficit Reduction Act of 1984 (H. R. 4170) froze physicians' fees for fifteen months beginning July 1, 1984. The legislation includes strong incentives to encourage physicians to accept assignment and not to bill the patient for charges above the Medicare allowance except for the usual coinsurance. In addition, the development of PPOs by private insurance companies and employers is spurring the negotiation of fees with individual physicians and physicians' groups.

Stimulation of Competition and the Entry of Venture Capital into the Health Field. For several years, a major debate has been under way in the health policy field between proponents of market forces in health care and those who believe that a truly price competitive market is not viable in this sector of our economy. The latter group believes that health is a merit good and that regulation is the only way to control costs.[15] The truth probably lies somewhere in between.

The increase in the supply of physicians, the entry of venture capital into the health field, and the growing influence of promarket advocates in the health care debate have stimulated a competitive environment and the growth of market forces. Evidence of this trend includes several developments. There has been a rapid expansion of HMOs—both for-profit and not-for-profit. In the past, a major barrier to HMO growth was the difficulty of recruiting and retaining physicians. With the growth in the supply of physicians this is no longer the case. Many other types of delivery settings are being developed as variations on physicians' offices. In addition, services that were formerly provided in hospitals on an inpatient basis are now moving outside the hospitals.[16] Examples include urgent care centers (substituting for physicians' offices and routine care in hospital emergency rooms); surgicenters for day surgery; diagnostic centers; birthing centers; and hospices. Home health care services are also expanding.

104

Other competitive developments include the growing influence of "venture capital" and for-profit corporations in the health service delivery field.[17] Furthermore, nonprofit hospitals are becoming entrepreneurial as evidenced through the formation of multihospital organizations, corporate reorganization, and development of for-profit subsidiaries. While for many years the trend has been to expand employment-based health insurance benefits and to reduce cost sharing, today this trend is being reversed. Recent studies conducted by the Rand Corporation indicate that increased cost sharing does exert a downward influence on utilization of services.[18]

All of these forces are affecting physicians and hospitals, setting physicians in competition with other physicians and with hospitals. It will take several years, however, before the long-range effects of increased physician supply, changes in reimbursement, and the growth of competition on utilization, costs, and quality of care are fully known.

The Corporatization of American Medicine—Profit and Nonprofit

The health industry in the past was characterized by numerous small- and medium-sized firms mainly nonprofit in nature. The more than 7,000 hospitals were independently owned and controlled. Solo or small group practice for physicians was the dominant practice pattern. Home health agencies were, for the most part, community-based individual agencies, usually visiting nurse services.

For-profit institutions and hospital chains and for-profit home health agencies did exist before the mid-1960s; but, except for the drug, device, and medical supply sectors, they constituted a very small proportion of the health industry. The passage of Medicare/ Medicaid in 1965, with the assurance of broader government financing of health care services, stimulated the growth of for-profit hospitals, nursing homes, renal dialysis centers, and home health agencies. Specifically, three features of Medicare payments to providers encouraged the growth of for-profit institutions: payment of interest on borrowing; return on equity; and payment of depreciation on the facilities, which could be revalued on sale. In the past twenty years, hospital chains and corporations have purchased facilities and services previously owned by individuals and small groups. Today, with the increased incentives to move services out of the hospital, similar patterns are emerging with the creation of HMOs, surgicenters, and urgent care centers.

The nonprofit hospital industry, which heretofore confined itself to the operation of single units and to hospital-based services, is now seeking to emulate the pattern of the for-profit sector. Multi-

105

hospital organizations are forming: hospitals are reorganizing and forming for-profit subsidiaries to provide products and services, and they are opening free-standing urgent care and surgicenters and are increasingly employing physicians. Both the for-profit and nonprofit sectors are offering management, financial, data, and purchasing services to other health providers.

With the growth in the supply of physicians, the increasing debt burden medical students incur for education, and the rising costs of private practice, young physicians have been seeking and accepting salaried arrangements in hospitals, HMOs, multispecialty group practices, and urgent care centers. The balance between the individual entrepreneur—the fee-for-service physician—and the corporate entrepreneur is shifting.

Such a shift and the growth of corporate health care imposes constraints on the autonomy of the physician. When physicians are employed by others, measures of productivity and cost-effective behavior become more dominant. Inevitably there will be a subtle shift in the weighting of values between the medical ethos that everything must be done for the patient and the bottom line of economic survival of a corporate structure and its share of the market. The tensions between patient well-being and economics will increase the tension between the physician and the corporate structure, whether the corporate structure is an HMO, a hospital, or another service provider. The physicians will also be subject to these tensions themselves. The economic incentives in some HMOs, for example, are to do less for the patient and to provide only necessary services, thereby maximizing the physician's share of profits.

Yet no corporate structure in health care can exist without physician services; and, over time, physicians can be expected to organize and negotiate for their medical care values and their share of the profits.

What is emerging is a change from multiple individual tensions and pressures to large-scale equivalents of labor-management or international negotiations. The corporate structure has moved more rapidly than physicians' consciousness of change, but physicians are now entering the marketplace and forming their own corporate structures. Today, we are witnessing this change most clearly in the field of ambulatory care.

The Hospital as Entrepreneur

The hospital industry is very diverse. There are more than 7,000 hospitals in the United States, and these can be clustered in numerous categories. Two categories, ownership/governance and mission, influence the degree to which the institutions can successfully engage in entrepreneurial activities.

Ownership and Governance. There are three basic nonfederal classes of hospital ownership—public, nonprofit voluntary, and for-profit. Each class has some subsets, which will be described briefly.

Public hospitals. State-owned hospitals, except for mental institutions, are generally owned by universities. Some of these hospitals serve as tertiary regional or state centers. Some, by charter or expectation of their legislatures, are required to accept all who need care regardless of financial status. Some are prohibited from engaging in competitive enterprises or from joining forces with other hospitals. Recently there has been a movement to change the governance structure of many of these institutions to enable them to meet competition from community hospitals.[19]

Many universities are sponsoring HMOs or entering into preferred provider arrangements, and the university itself is stimulating faculty to increase their attention to patient care activities to retain their share of the market.

Several factors, however, are likely to impede the ability of these institutions to be highly competitive. The costs of educating house staff, medical students, and students in other health professions make these hospitals more expensive than community hospitals. Faculty who admit and care for patients in these institutions are expected to function in multiple roles rather than concentrate their efforts on caring for patients or on keeping costs down. Their academic rewards are based on teaching skills, research productivity, and continuing-education activities, as well as on clinical excellence. The mixed missions of the faculty and the hospitals, as well as exogenous government constraints, limit the degree of entrepreneurial endeavor.

County and municipal hospitals are tax supported to provide care for the indigent and medically needy. Although Medicare and Medicaid enabled many of these hospitals to reduce their dependence on county and municipal revenues and to expand their base of paying patients, most of these hospitals still provide a disproportionate amount of uncompensated care. Many of the larger county and municipal hospitals are also large teaching hospitals.

Their mission, ownership, constraints on personnel, purchasing, arrangements with other facilities, and prohibitions on profitmaking endeavors limit their enterpreneurial ability. Governance changes to allow increased entrepreneurial prospects need to be weighed against

107

the risks of reducing indigents' access and of stopping the flow of county and municipal funds for indigent care.

Nonprofit voluntary hospitals. This group is composed of hospitals diverse by every measure: size, teaching status, mission, and governance. By and large they are more flexible than public hospitals in their ability to enter into agreements with other institutions, engage in corporate reorganization, or make changes in patient mix and mission.

Great activity is occurring in this group of hospitals in several areas. Many of these hospitals are undergoing corporate reorganization and are developing for-profit subsidiaries. They are entering multiorganizational arrangements with similar institutions and are developing ambulatory services, such as freestanding urgent care centers, surgicenters, HMOs, and PPOs.

With the exception of the nonprofit teaching hospitals, these voluntary institutions have open staffs, compete for admissions, and cannot easily organize physicians into multispecialty groups nor easily control physicians' ordering practices within the hospital. Given the increased supply of physicians, however, prestigious institutions, sole community providers, and dominant community hospitals could begin to develop closed staff arrangements and market the full range of ambulatory services under contract with physicians' groups.

For-profit hospitals. Initially, for-profit hospitals were small hospitals owned by physicians or local business groups. During the past twenty years, investor-owned companies have entered the market at a growing rate, purchasing single ownership hospitals and building new ones. Many of the hospital corporations have contracts to manage nonprofit hospitals.

In terms of competition, these hospitals have few of the constraints characteristic of public and nonprofit hospitals. Few provide care for the indigent, unless they are sole community providers. When they are not the sole community provider, they may select not to provide certain services that lose money, such as obstetrics and pediatrics. Few provide community tertiary care services like burn or trauma centers and neonatal intensive care. They are rarely teaching hospitals, although recently some for-profit companies have purchased or leased major teaching hospitals. Most important, they can raise capital more readily than their nonprofit counterparts. These hospitals have been the most aggressive in responding to changes in the market and to changes in supply and reimbursement. Many of them are setting up home health services, urgent care centers, surgicenters, HMOs, and insurance companies.

Mission. The mission and the history of an institution will also influence its response to change. Many nonprofit hospitals are community based with longstanding missions of serving the needs of a specific geographic area. They are dependent on the community for support in use of the facility, capital funding including public bonds, and deficit financing for care of community indigents.

Other nonprofits have strong identification with religious groups as well as histories of serving certain population groups such as the indigent. Boards of trustees of some of these institutions are reluctant to change established patterns, even when the institutions become nonsectarian over time. Some of the most aggressive activity, however, in forming multiorganizational arrangements has occurred with Catholic, Lutheran, and Methodist hospitals.

The mission of some state university and county municipal hospitals to care for the indigent also affects their ability to compete with other hospitals and with physicians. Education and research, too, are real costs that affect the price the hospital charges for service. Currently no mechanism exists for spreading these costs among all hospitals.

Costs for the substantial pool of patients who can pay nothing or only a partial amount for their care are passed on through the hospital's charge structure to other payers or to states and counties. The changes in reimbursement and the formation of PPOs are stimulating a shift of uncompensated care patients to public and certain nonprofit teaching hospitals. As nonprofit hospitals reduce uncompensated care and also begin to reduce money-losing services, greater and greater proportions of uncompensated care will shift to public hospitals. The result may be deterioration in services and in the capital plant of the public institutions, restricting access to care for certain population groups.

Teaching. As reimbursement for hospital care has become more restrictive and as competition has increased, the size of some hospital teaching programs has slightly declined.[20] While the debate over the costs of education borne by hospitals and the tradeoffs between education and quality of patient care in a highly competitive environment continues, as costs and price become dominant factors, there are clear incentives to reduce the teaching commitment within institutions.

Although the decline in some residency positions has not yet had a major impact, indications are that this trend will accelerate. Teaching hospitals also serve as sites of training for nursing, dental, pharmacy, and allied health students. Reductions have already been noted in training for clinical pharmacists and nurses.[21]

109

There are two reasons that many teaching institutions may have an advantage in developing and organizing total systems of care, extending far beyond hospital inpatient services. First, most of the major teaching hospitals have large organized physician staffs with practice plan arrangements already in place. Second, because of their teaching mission they have a wide diversity of physician and other health professional skills. As discussed before, however, constraints on competitiveness make it difficult to organize vertical systems rapidly.

The purpose of the above description is to indicate that hospitals, because of several factors, will respond differentially to competition and that conclusions about hospitals as a whole should not be drawn without careful analysis of the hospitals involved and their context.

The Physician as Entrepreneur

Most physicians in private practice have always been entrepreneurs who seek to maximize income or profit.[22] In salaried practice, bonuses for productivity or volume are quite common. The percentage arrangements made by pathologists, radiologists, and anesthesiologists are clearly examples of the physician as a business-person.

Until the recent rapid increase in the supply of physicians, the physician could, with few inhibitions, choose his type of practice, site of practice, specialty, hospital base, hours of work, fees, and benefits. The hospital, the consumer, and the insurer had little control over physicians' medical decisions and their consequences on utilization or cost.

During the 1950s and 1960s, the demand for services exceeded the supply of physicians. In many parts of the country, physicians ceased making house calls, ended weekend and evening hours, and left primary care practice for specialization. The growth of HMOs was slowed by the unwillingness of physicians to work in salaried settings.

When the supply of physicians was limited, hospitals needed to attract competent staff. To ensure their financial viability, hospitals acceded to most demands of physicians for equipment and ancillary services.

The large investment in medical education and the expansion of enrollment in the 1960s and 1970s has now reversed the supply and demand picture. The 1980 report of the Graduate Medical Education National Advisory Committee projected a 40 percent increase in the physician supply between 1978 and 1990 and forecast a 70,000 physician surplus. Newly graduating physicians are finding it more difficult to locate in areas of geographic preference and to start solo or small group practices. As a result, they are more willing than their predecessors to accept salaried positions. The increased supply of physicians, the decline in hospital admissions, and the reduced length of stay, combined with the new reimbursement policies for hospitals, will have a profound effect on hospital and physician relations.

DRG reimbursement has already begun to limit the freedom of the physician to order hospital services. The changes in hospital payment are also strengthening hospitals' bargaining positions vis-à-vis physicians for running laboratory, X-ray, and other services within the hospital. The increased supply of physicians will allow hospitals to use admitting privileges to reinforce the incentives in the new reimbursement methods. There are countervailing pressures, however, including increased competition among hospitals for "stars"—preeminent physicians who can attract many patients. Physicians, hospitals, and corporations have increased their efforts to gain control of services that can be provided on an inpatient or outpatient basis, such as noninvasive diagnostic imaging; laboratory and X-ray services for preadmission testing; urgent care; home health care; and a host of technologically oriented services that can be provided in multiple settings, such as dialysis, chemotherapy, total parenteral nutrition, and plasmapheresis.

Several additional factors will affect these relations: the entry of corporate for-profit firms (that is, hospitals, investor groups, and health care manufacturers); the ability of physicians to raise capital; and the ability of the nonprofit hospital sector to raise capital to finance out-of-hospital services.

Current hospital reimbursement and certificate-of-need legislation in most states provide incentives to move many of the hospital services that can be provided on an inpatient or outpatient basis into free-standing facilities that are not subject to certificate of need. The degree of physician control will depend on whether physicians themselves can raise the capital and manage these services or whether they will work for corporations and hospitals who own and manage these services. The ability of physicians to organize and negotiate for their share of the health care pie also influences the dynamics.

The increased supply of physicians, combined with the pressures on hospitals to constrain physician activity, will lead to conflict within the hospital walls and to greater efforts of physicians to control services and the mode of practice. It will also lead to increased competition and conflict among physicians and between physicians and other health professionals. In the United States, physicians are licensed in a way that allows them to practice not only their own specialties but others as well. This phenomenon will stimulate competition between primary care physicians and specialists; among specialties with overlapping skills; between physicians and other health professionals, such as nurse practitioners, podiatrists, physician assistants, physiotherapists, and clinical pharmacists.

As in the case of the different types of hospitals, effects and responses will vary by factors such as geographic location, age of established practice, specialty, hospital capacity, competition, and availability of capital.

Conclusions

Predicting the future is extremely difficult, particularly with little past experience on which to draw. For almost fifty years the following conditions existed:

• a perceived shortage of physicians and considerable autonomy of physicians in choice of practice, specialty, and location; negotiations with hospitals; and price of services

• expansion of hospital plant and technology with few financial constraints, allowing hospitals and physicians to develop income-enhancing relations

• growth of third-party payments, reducing the cost-consciousness of providers and consumers

• increased federal and state investment to pay for care for the poor and elderly on an almost open-ended basis

• advances in technology that increased utilization and costs

The health sector has now entered a new era; expansion is being replaced by constraints. Tensions inherent in redistributing a more finite set of resources have begun and are bound to increase. This new era is characterized by

• an increased supply of physician manpower and growing competition among physicians

• excess hospital capacity, declining hospital utilization, and constraints on payment with increased interhospital competition and competition between hospitals and physicians

• increased entry of venture capital, corporations, and for-profit entities in what was a nonprofit dominated industry that has been followed by changes in the behavior of nonprofit enterprises in order to compete

• changes in health insurance coverage increasing the cost for consumers at the time of service

• development of new health care delivery modes, systems of care, and payment mechanisms

With the formation of new relations among health professionals, hospitals, and other providers, a decade of turbulence can be anticipated. There is only one safe prediction: Neither physicians nor hospitals will continue to enjoy the same degree of autonomy in decisions affecting the consumer and the public that they have enjoyed in the past.

Notes

1. Paul Starr, *The Social Transformation of American Medicine* (New York: Basic Books, 1982).

2. Michael Zubkoff, ed., *Health: A Victim or Cause of Inflation* (New York: Prodist, 1976).

3. Institute of Medicine, *Costs of Education in the Health Professions* (Washington, D.C.: National Academy of Sciences, 1974), chapter 1.

4. U.S. Department of Health and Human Services, Health Resources Administration, *Summary Report of the Graduate Medical Education National Advisory Committee*, DHHS (HRA) 81–651 (September 1980).

5. "83rd Annual Report on Medical Education in the United States, 1982–83," *Journal of the American Medical Association* (September 23, 1983), p. 250.

6. William D. Schwartz, et al., "The Changing Geographic Distribution of Board Certified Physicians," *New England Journal of Medicine* (October 30, 1980), pp. 1032–38.

7. "Socioeconomic Characteristics of Medical Practice," American Medical Association (1983).

8. Herman M. Somers and Anne R. Somers, *Medicare and the Hospitals* (Washington, D.C.: Brookings Institution, 1967).

9. Zubkoff, *Health: A Victim or Cause of Inflation*.

10. Social Security Amendments (1983).

11. Tax Equity and Fiscal Responsibility Act (1982).

12. Bruce C. Vladeck, "Medicare Payment by Diagnostic Related Groups," *Annals of Internal Medicine*, vol. 100 (April 1984), pp. 576–91.

13. Ibid.

14. Victor R. Fuchs, "The Battle for Control of Health Care," *Health Affairs*, vol. 1 (Summer 1982); John H. Moxley III and Penelope C. Roeder, "New Opportunities for Out-of-Hospital Health Services," *New England Journal of Medicine*, vol. 310 (January 19, 1984), pp. 193–97.

15. Institute of Medicine, "Controls on Health Care," *Papers of the Conference on Regulation in the Health Industry, January 7–9, 1974* (Washington, D.C.: National Academy of Sciences, 1975).

16. Ruth S. Hanft, "Alternatives to Hospital Care," prepared for Work in America Institute Meeting, Washington, D.C., May 9, 1984.

17. Arnold S. Relman, M.D., "The New Medical Industrial Complex," *New England Journal of Medicine*, vol. 303 (October 23, 1980), pp. 963–70.

18. J. P. Newhouse, W. G. Manning, C. N. Morris, et al., "Some Interim Results from a Controlled Trial of Cost Sharing in Health Insurance," *New England Journal of Medicine*, vol. 305 (December 17, 1981), pp. 1501–1507.

19. Fred Munson, Robert Allison, and Thomas Choi, *Management and Governance of University Hospitals*, Consortium for the Study of University Hospitals, July 1983.

20. Ruth S. Hanft and Renee Heyman, *Impact of Changes in Federal Policy on Academic Health Centers* (Washington, D.C.: Association of Academic Health Centers, October 1982).

21. Ibid.

22. Starr, *Social Transformation*; Fuchs, "Battle for Control."

7

The Static Dynamics of Long-Term Care Policy

Bruce C. Vladeck

The development of long-term care policy in the United States has entered a curious stage. Consensus among members of the policy community about many of the key issues in program design is probably greater than it has been in many years. The body of knowledge about long-term care clients, services, and financing is certainly greater than at any previous time and is still growing. Yet the aversion of the current national administration to any innovation in domestic policy other than the renunciation of federal responsibilities has blocked not only efforts at systematic policy reform but even small-scale experimentation. At the same time, the increasingly vigorous discussions of the future of Medicare generally ignore—often by quite explicit choice—long-term care issues that are critically dependent on Medicare policy and that are also likely to influence the effectiveness of Medicare policy changes.

At one level the current stasis in long-term care policy reflects primarily the inability of policy makers productively to address fiscal conflict between the federal and state governments; President Reagan's New Federalism initiative appears to have led this perpetual dialogue into a dead end rather than into new initiatives. Which level of government will get stuck with the bills has indeed been a major axis around which long-term care policy has revolved for some time, and the issue needs to be addressed in some way if we are to move off the multibillion-dollar dime. Other principles are at stake, however; and the current policy stalemate may arise from conflicts about the appropriate roles of government, families, and individual responsibility so profound that only creative and aggressive policy leadership, of a kind now nowhere to be found, can end it.

In a brief discussion such as this one, it is hard to do justice to all aspects of this complex puzzle. As has always been the case, long-term care hangs on the end of the line in a kind of great social game of crack the whip: what actually happens to clients and providers is as likely to be the result of unintended consequences of Medicare, or social security, or income maintenance policy as of conscious efforts to reform long-term care. So, rather than attempting a synoptic analysis, I will try in this paper to explain where we are, and perhaps where we should be going, in a narrative, quasi-chronological fashion. What follows is thus as much an exercise in informal intellectual history as in policy analysis.

Nursing Homes

As recently as the late 1970s, defining the long-term care problem and options for dealing with it seemed relatively simple. Formal long-term care services were provided overwhelmingly in nursing homes, a type of institution that had essentially not existed a quarter of a century earlier but that had proliferated enormously since then. In 1977 roughly 1.1 million elderly Americans resided in some 18,000 nursing homes, receiving services that were widely perceived to be qualitatively inferior, personally demoralizing, and—for a significant fraction of residents—excessively and inappropriately medical. Roughly half of nursing home care was financed by public sources—almost entirely Medicaid—comprising more than 90 percent of all public long-term care expenditures. In the first six or seven years of the 1970s, nursing home care had been, by a considerable margin, the fastest-growing object of Medicaid expenditures; Medicaid had, in turn, been the fastest-growing item in many state budgets.[1]

Moreover there appeared to be no end in sight. Given the inexorable demographic trends, including the increasing numbers of the elderly and the increasing proportion of the very old among the elderly (since nursing home use is overwhelmingly a phenomenon of those seventy-five and older), continued dramatic expansion of nursing home services was anticipated. That expansion of services was, of course, expected to bring with it a concomitant growth in expenditures. The Congressional Budget Office, for example, in a 1977 study, projected the addition of one million new beds, at an annual cost in excess of $20 billion, by the end of the century.[2]

Expansion of in-home services seemed to be the only solution. Several studies, performed in different ways in different communities at different times, suggested that much nursing home use was inappropriate; that is, depending on the study, anywhere from 10 to 40 percent of nursing home patients evaluated were deemed capable of remaining in the community, if adequate services and supports were provided.[3] Since the conventional wisdom held that in-home care was significantly cheaper than institutional care, caring for those inappropriately placed in nursing homes in alternative settings was expected both to enhance quality and to reduce costs.

Since 1977 or 1978, something remarkable appears to have happened. Without any conscious policy direction at the national level, we appear as a nation to have almost stopped building nursing homes. A recent study by the General Accounting Office, the first systematic updating of any kind since the mid-1970s on trends in nursing home capacity, concludes that, since 1977, the supply of nursing home beds has grown at a pace roughly equal to the increase in the over-sixty-five population and thus more slowly than the key over-seventy-five population.[4] The GAO almost certainly overestimates the growth in supply because of the difficulty in separating from state statistics the intermediate care facilities for the mentally retarded (ICF/MRs) and the custodial facilities for the nonelderly, deinstitutionalized mentally ill. At a minimum, however, clearly the growth in capacity has slowed dramatically since the mid-1970s, contrary to most expectations at the time.

The reasons for that slowdown are not entirely clear—especially since hardly anyone realized it was happening. Certificate-of-need programs had some effect, especially after the implementation of the 1974 Planning Act (P.L. 93–641) in 1976 and thereafter. So had reimbursement policies, as states, after scandals in New York and elsewhere in the mid-1970s, cracked down on the profits that had been available from real estate trafficking and other means of manipulating Medicaid reimbursement.[5] High interest rates, however, undoubtedly also played a role in an industry that had traditionally been financed by conventional mortgage debt. And the general bad aura enveloping nursing homes following the scandals must have further discouraged both existing and potential operators, as well as local zoning boards and lending institutions.

At the same time the institutional bed supply was being constrained, in-home services grew enormously. That growth was, in part, the result of conscious national policy initiatives. Medicare home health benefits expanded in both 1980 and 1981; and 1981 legislation encouraged the expansion of Medicaid benefits. Since the late 1970s, home health care has been the fastest-growing category of Medicare expenditures, with a compound annual growth rate in excess of 20 percent.[6] Reliable data on the capacity of home-health providers is almost completely nonexistent, but capacity appears to have grown in parallel with utilization.

Home health care will be further discussed below. To return for a moment to the discussion of nursing homes, it is widely believed, with some evidence to support the belief, that supply constraints in a context of demographic trends have led to a significant increase in average severity and dependency levels among nursing home residents. At the same time, in many communities arranging nursing home placements for "heavy care" patients who lack the ability to pay premium rates appears increasingly difficult.[7] These two phenomena may at first appear contradictory, but the apparent contradiction is resolved by two other phenomena. The first is that, as far as anyone can tell, nursing home residents are living longer after admission, a result both of somewhat improved nursing home care and, especially, of continuing development in medical technology. The other phenomenon is that, again at least in some places, although obtaining nursing home admissions for the most disabled patients is harder, admissions of the least disabled have been reduced. That reduction may, in turn, result from strengthened formal controls on the appropriateness of admissions, the expansion of noninstitutional long-term care services, and growing consumer awareness of the availability of noninstitutional forms of care.

Yet, although the characteristics of nursing home patients may be changing and the supply of beds has been constrained, there have been few innovations in formal policy regarding nursing homes. Efforts to reform substantially the process by which the quality of nursing home care is defined and regulated, initiated at the federal level in the early 1970s, were sidetracked by the change in administrations in 1981 at the point of adoption. A subsequent effort to deregulate the industry was beaten back by well-organized consumer and congressional resistance eighteen months later. The whole issue was then kicked to the Institute of Medicine, which is due to issue its report in mid-1985. The Health Care Financing Administration (HCFA) is having difficulty developing a proposal for Medicare prospective payment for skilled nursing facilities, as it has been required to do by Congress, notwithstanding that Medicare pays for less than 3 percent of nursing home days, while Medicaid, which pays for more than half of nursing home days, has long had prospective payment in many states.

Meanwhile, more fundamental questions about where nursing homes belong in a health care system increasingly dominated by geriatric patients, or what kind of institutions they should be, are largely unaddressed, at least at the national policy level. The problems of quality assurance, inadequate professional involvement, high costs, and appropriateness of patient populations remain about what they were a decade ago. Worse, although the professional literature is continually increasing and informative, reliable hard data about nursing homes and their patients are remarkably sparse. To take two examples, a single, reliable count of how many nursing home beds there are in the United States does not exist, and the estimates of nursing home expenditures contained in HCFA's annual report on national health expenditures are still based on 1977 survey data updated by trend factors.[8]

Home Health

About the same time in the late 1970s that policy analysts were calling for expanded in-home services as an alternative to nursing homes, researchers were documenting an important, related phenomenon, the implications of which have still not been fully recognized. Most disabled elderly persons in need of regular and continuing assistance with activities of daily living (a good working definition of those in need of long-term care) were already getting it at home, largely from spouses, daughters, or daughters-in-law. Although some of the demand for nursing home care arose from families "dumping" elderly relatives, most nursing home residents had no immediate family member capable of taking care of them. Far more striking, both statistically and emotionally, were the sacrifices of millions of family members. Continuing research has consistently shown that between two-thirds and three-quarters of the disabled elderly are cared for at home with few or no formal services.[9]

This phenomenon has two significant sets of implications for the expansion of in-home services, which are indeed contradictory. First, although people tend to fear and resist institutionalization for themselves and their relatives, they appear to welcome the increased availability of formal services in the home for which someone else pays. Thus, while public subsidies for nursing home care do not, by and large, substitute for the care a family gives, public subsidies for home care well may. Public programs are thus at substantial risk of drawing on an enormous pool of latent demand if benefits are expanded. Second, the evidence about the successful maintenance of severely disabled people in their own or relatives' homes for protracted periods suggests that, with appropriate motivation and supports in the home, elaborately equipped facilities are not required for the rendering of satisfactory care. Home care is thus a techno-logically feasible alternative even for the seriously disabled.

Whether or not home care is a less expensive alternative appar-ently depends on just how it is provided, in what kind of community, and for what kind of client. Under the best of circumstances—setting aside, for the moment, the latent demand issue—satisfactory home care is considerably less expensive than satisfactory nursing home care, especially if housing costs are somehow removed from the equation on the home care side and the value of services performed by friends and relatives are not included in the accounting. The best of circumstances rarely prevail, however, and the diseconomies of small scale are particularly consequential for home care. Accounting for all costs, regardless of who pays them, and controlling for types of cases, home care is sometimes cheaper than nursing home care and sometimes not.[10]

From a public policy perspective, given a *ceteris paribus* preference for noninstitutional services, a way to deal with this kind of "it depends" phenomenon would be to provide coverage for in-home services in those instances in which home care can be provided at an expense no greater than institutional care. Beginning with New York's "Nursing Home without Walls" legislation in 1978, policy has indeed been going in that direction. If a patient would otherwise be eligible for Medicaid-reimbursed nursing home care and can be satisfactorily cared for at home for a monthly expense no greater than 75 percent of the prevailing nursing home rate, then Medicaid will pay for those services in the home. That was the logic of New York's legislation, which then became the model for section 2176 of the 1981 Omnibus Reconciliation Act, which provided for so-called home and community-based waivers for long-term care Medicaid clients.

This logic contains one potentially fatal flaw. Although one may be able to determine, under a particular set of circumstances, which clients might be eligible for nursing home care, as a practical matter determining who will actually *receive* nursing home care is very different. Eligibility is not synonomous with receipt of services, particularly because the medical and functional definitions of service "need" are notoriously subjective and manipulable and because most Medicaid residents of nursing homes are first admitted as privately paying patients, who then "spend down" to Medicaid eligibility. Moreover, in a situation in which demand exceeds supply, as it generally does for nursing homes, some who truly are eligible will not get in.

Put another way, it is hard to insure that public agencies will save money by diverting patients from institutional to community-based services so long as those agencies control only part of the queue for nursing home admission. In the worst case, one can envision a situation in which all those clients poor enough to qualify for Medicaid while residing in the community are diverted to in-home services with the most seriously disabled placed in acute hospital beds, whereas nursing home admissions are available only to patients with the resources to pay privately—many of whom will then spend down to Medicaid eligibility, something much easier to achieve once one is in a nursing home.

The policy response to that problem is to attempt to create a single queue by applying uniform criteria to all nursing-home admissions. As a practical matter, the easiest way to do that without running into legal or constitutional obstacles is to deny spend-down Medicaid eligibility to anyone who has previously been admitted to a nursing home without the same preadmission screening applied to those already eligible for Medicaid, while forbidding nursing homes from discharging those patients whose resources are thereby exhausted. Such a plan has been adopted in Virginia and, more recently, in South Carolina.

Perhaps more to the point, while in-home or community-based services may be cheaper than institutional care for many individuals (as well as being qualitatively preferable in many cases), it is not *enough* cheaper to completely nullify the effects of growing demand arising from demographic trends, technological change, and changes in family composition. Even if measures can somehow be found to limit the extent to which latent demand is tapped, expanding in-home services can only shave the rate of growth in total expenditures, not eliminate the growth.

Still, in-home services, both in private and public markets, grow like Topsy. As was the case with nursing homes a generation ago, such growth creates serious potential problems of quality assurance, professional training, service organization and coordination, and financial control. None of these problems appear to be receiving much serious scrutiny, certainly not at the federal level. The next generation of scandals is probably waiting to happen.

Medicare

Expenditures for skilled nursing facilities and acute home health services comprise less than 3 percent of all Medicare Part A costs. Although Part B home health and related expenses have grown substantially in recent years, they still fall below 5 percent of Part B expenditures.[11] The administrator of the Health Care Financing Administration has stated on many occasions that Medicare does not cover long-term care services. Discussions of the future of Medicare triggered by reports of the impending bankruptcy of the Hospital Insurance Trust Fund have generally ignored long-term care issues, except to assume or imply that a larger Medicare role is unaffordable.

Yet Medicare is implicated in the long-term care system to a far greater extent than is generally recognized, and it is hard to see how the long-term care system can be straightened out without Medicare's playing an appropriate part.

First, Medicare pays for many services to long-term care clients who have never been systematically identified as such. The biggest dollar amount is probably incurred by the 3 to 7 percent of all Medicare "acute" hospital days that involve patients on "alternate care" status awaiting nursing home placement.[12] A significant, but unknown, number of Medicare hospital admissions are from nursing homes, often related to inadequate or insufficient nursing home care. Most physician visits to nursing home and home care patients are billed to Part B. Essentially all over-sixty-five nursing home residents are, after all, Medicare beneficiaries, even if Medicare is not paying the nursing home directly.

At the same time, the adoption of diagnosis-related-group (DRG)-based prospective payment for Medicare hospital services is widely predicted to increase pressures on hospitals to arrange earlier discharges to nursing homes or home care, while accelerating the already existing trends to vertical integration of hospitals into nursing home or home care services. The notion that increased expenditures for post-acute services will negate Medicare savings from prospective payment seems rather farfetched, but it does seem likely that any savings resulting from quicker movement of patients through the system will redound to the hospitals, not to Medicare.

Medicaid

Medicaid, meanwhile, continues to hold the bag, as the provider of catastrophic and long-term care insurance to Medicare beneficiaries. The generally cited figures are that Medicaid pays for about half of nursing home care (constituting, in the process, between 35 and 40 percent of total Medicaid expenditures) but, for various reasons, Medicaid actually pays, at any given time, for more than two-thirds of nursing-home days. The discrepancy between Medicaid's share of expenses and its share of days arises from two phenomena. First, Medicaid is a *net* payer, paying the balance between the rates it allows and the client's monthly income, and essentially all nursing home residents have social security income. Second, private rates are higher—often considerably higher—than Medicaid's. By law, they can be no lower.[13]

The ramifications of Medicaid's role in long-term care and the increasingly sophisticated efforts of state policy makers to grapple with them are sufficiently complex to merit an entirely separate discussion. For purposes of the current paper, just two essential points need to be made. First is the nearly total interdependence of Medicare and Medicaid policies as they involve long-term care clients; when Medicare sneezes, Medicaid catches pneumonia. Second is the bizarre character of the Medicaid eligibility process for most long-term care clients. To oversimplify only slightly, Medicaid coverage of long-term care is provided largely to formerly middle-class people who have been totally impoverished by medical and related expenses and is much more readily available to people already in nursing homes than equally poor and disabled people not in them. Not only is Medicaid the payer of last resort, but also its fiscal liability is determined primarily by providers and potential clients entirely outside its jurisdiction. The ability of Medicaid programs to take control of their own destinies in long-term care is thus highly constrained.

Insurance

Given these constraints on Medicaid and the constantly increasing demand, there is a growing body of sentiment that future financing of long-term care will increasingly have to depend on new forms of private insurance. This sentiment is reinforced by the expectation that the elderly will be more affluent, at least in relative terms, in coming years and by ideological predispositions toward private sector solutions. A recent conference sponsored by HCFA on future policy options for financing long-term care focused almost exclusively, for example, on private insurance mechanisms, and both academics and insurance companies have undertaken several studies of potential insurance schemes. The most plausible of such schemes provide for fixed monthly premiums beginning somewhere between age fifty and age sixty-five and indemnity-style long-term care benefits with substantial deductibles and coinsurance.[14]

Unfortunately, there are four major problems with private long-term care insurance. First, although the elderly are, on average, increasingly better off, those most at risk for future long-term care services are the least well-off among the elderly, who continue to be quite marginal economically. Like many forms of insurance, long-term care insurance is most affordable for those who least need it. Second, it is not at all clear that long-term care is the kind of risk that is truly insurable. There is too much discretion involved in defining service "need," too much risk of "moral hazard," in which the availability of services of insurance encourages use and self-selection by higher-risk clients. Third, it is hard to make long-term care insurance policies both actuarially sound—especially given the preceding point—and economically attractive. The hypothetical plans now being discussed offer surprisingly limited benefits for the premiums they require. Finally—on an issue insurance industry representatives identify as the most important barrier to private insurance—Medicaid already serves as a catastrophic insurer of last resort for the middle class.[15] In other words, to put their hopes on the private insurance mechanism, public officials have to hope that their constituents will be dumb enough to make an irrational investment to reduce their potential consumption of tax dollars.

Integration

Of course, many—literally uncounted billions—private dollars are already in the long-term care system. The interplay between public and private dollars is not, however, very productive or rational from anyone's perspective. Better ways need to be found to mesh public and private dollars.

At the same time, however, we know there need to be better ways to mesh informal and formal services and better ways to maximize the benefit—both qualitative and economic—of interservice tradeoffs. Better care of elderly patients in acute hospitals reduces the demand for nursing home care just as better nursing home care reduces the need for readmission to acute hospitals. Institutionalization may be prevented by providing family caregivers with occasional respite or relief services. Patients sick enough to be in nursing homes can be kept at home with targeted formal services—if public dollars are available. But the disjunction of funding streams, with the all-or-nothing, impoverishment-requiring character of Medicaid eligibility at the core of the issue, often makes such meshing of services impossible.

The most promising concrete effort to confront these problems directly involves the planned demonstration of Social/Health Maintenance Organizations (SHMOs). The four SHMOs' implementation will be financed by capitation at 100 percent of the areawide average adjusted per capita cost (AAPCC) for Medicare, plus a monthly premium competitive with standard Medigap policies for those who can afford it, or an equivalent Medicaid rate for those poor enough to qualify for Medicaid in the community. At this price, the SHMOs would provide the full range of existing Part A and B Medicare benefits, expanded acute benefits (notably prescription drugs and eyeglasses), and a range of long-term care benefits, with a particular emphasis on case management and in-home care, all under the discipline of fixed prepayment. The sponsors of the SHMOs contend that at those rates SHMOs can provide such a range of services to a broadly representative population of the elderly and still break even, or better, because the combination of prepayment incentives, unified funding, case management, and a broad range of available services will permit them to substitute less-expensive for more-expensive services. In particular, they anticipate reductions in inpatient hospital utilization of as much as 25 percent.

Although development of the SHMOs was largely financed by HCFA, the full test of the concept was delayed for almost a year by the simple refusal of the federal Office of Management and Budget to approve the necessary Medicare waivers. It quite literally took an act of Congress to permit the SHMO demonstrations to go forward.[16] The OMB is obviously afraid of something. One suspects that it fears most of all a success that will make it more difficult for the federal government to wash its hands of responsibility for long-term care.

Probably no one system of financing and providing service is best for all clients in all communities. SHMOs may not even be an answer. Only a reasonable test can establish whether or not they are. The central components of the answer, however, are relatively clear: unified financing; integration of service systems, especially across the barrier between acute and long-term care; integration of formal and informal supports; and some form of case management under budgetary constraints, provided by independent professionals, service organizations, or family members. To assemble those components into an appropriate package, either at the specific local level or as more general national policy, there needs to be a prior political commitment to solving the problem without passing the buck to someone else. Little evidence of any such commitment in Washington now exists. As long as that situation prevails, so will policy stasis.

Notes

1. Cf. U.S. Congress, Congressional Budget Office, *Long-Term Care for the Elderly and Disabled* (Washington, D.C.: Government Printing Office, February 1977).

2. Ibid.

3. Ibid., Appendix B, pp. 55–58.

4. U.S. General Accounting Office, "Medicaid and Nursing Home Care: Cost Increases and the Need for Services Are Creating Problems for the States and the Elderly" (October 21, 1983), pp. 56–82.

5. Judith Feder and William Scanlon, "Regulating the Bed Supply in Nursing Homes," *The Milbank Memorial Fund Quarterly*, vol. 58 (1980), pp. 54–88.

6. U.S. General Accounting Office, "The Elderly Should Benefit from Expanded Home Health Care but Increasing These Services Will Not Insure Cost Reductions" (December 7, 1982).

7. General Accounting Office, "Medicaid and Nursing Home Care," pp. 26–33.

8. Robert M. Gibson, Daniel R. Waldo, and Katherine R. Levit, "National Health Expenditures, 1982," *Health Care Financing Review*, vol. 5 (Fall 1983), p. 28.

9. Bruce C. Vladeck, *Unloving Care: The Nursing Home Tragedy* (New York: Basic Books, 1980), pp. 16–17.

10. General Accounting Office, "The Elderly Should Benefit,"

11. "National Health Expenditures, 1982," p. 25.

12. General Accounting Office, "Medicaid and Nursing Home Care," pp. 110–27.

13. Vladeck, *Unloving Care*, p. 273.

14. Cf. Health Insurance Association, "Long Term Care: The Challenge to Society (HIAA)," 1984, p. 4.

15. Ibid.

16. P.L. 98–369, Sec. 2355.

A NOTE ON THE BOOK

This book was edited by S. Ellen Dykes of the
Publications Staff of the American Enterprise Institute.
Eason Associates, Inc., designed the cover, and
Hördur Karlsson drew the figure.
The text was set in Palatino, a typeface designed by Hermann Zapf.
EPS Group Inc., of Baltimore, Maryland, set the type, and
Edwards Brothers, of Ann Arbor, Michigan, printed and bound the book,
using acid-free Glatfelter Natural paper.

SELECTED AEI PUBLICATIONS

Evaluating State Medicaid Reforms, Pamela L. Haynes (1985, 36 pp., $4.95)

Incentives vs. Controls in Health Policy: Broadening the Debate, Jack A. Meyer, ed. (1985, 156 pp., cloth $15.95, paper $7.95)

Securing a Safer Blood Supply: Two Views, Ross D. Eckert and Edward L. Wallace, (1985, 153 pp., cloth $16.95, paper $8.95)

Medicaid Reform: Four Studies of Case Management, Deborah A. Freund, with Polly M. Ehrenhaft and Marie Hackbarth (1984, 83 pp., paper $5.95)

Managing Health Care Costs: Private Sector Innovations, Sean Sullivan, ed., with Polly M. Ehrenhaft (1984, 106 pp., cloth $15.95, paper $7.95)

Controlling Medicaid Costs: Federalism, Competition, and Choice, Thomas W. Grannemann and Mark V. Pauly (1983, 112 pp., cloth $13.95, paper $4.95)

Passing the Health Care Buck: Who Pays the Hidden Cost? Jack A. Meyer, with William R. Johnson and Sean Sullivan (1983, 49 pp., $3.95)

Market Reforms in Health Care: Current Issues, New Directions, Strategic Decisions, Jack A. Meyer, ed. (1983, 331 pp., cloth $19.95, paper $10.95)

• *Mail orders for publications to:* AMERICAN ENTERPRISE INSTITUTE, 1150 Seventeenth Street, N.W., Washington, D.C. 20036 • *For postage and handling, add 10 percent of total; minimum charge $2, maximum $10 (no charge on prepaid orders) • For information on orders, or to expedite service, call toll free 800-424-2873 (in Washington, D.C., 202-862-5869) • Prices subject to change without notice. • Payable in U.S. currency through U.S. banks only*

AEI ASSOCIATES PROGRAM

The American Enterprise Institute invites your participation in the competition of ideas through its AEI Associates Program. This program has two objectives: (1) to extend public familiarity with contemporary issues; and (2) to increase research on these issues and disseminate the results to policy makers, the academic community, journalists, and others who help shape public policies. The areas studied by AEI include Economic Policy, Education Policy, Energy Policy, Fiscal Policy, Government Regulation, Health Policy, International Programs, Legal Policy, National Defense Studies, Political and Social Processes, and Religion, Philosophy, and Public Policy. For the $49 annual fee, Associates receive

- a subscription to *Memorandum*, the newsletter on all AEI activities
- the AEI publications catalog and all supplements
- a 30 percent discount on all AEI books
- a 40 percent discount for certain seminars on key issues
- subscriptions to any two of the following publications: *Public Opinion*, a bimonthly magazine exploring trends and implications of public opinion on social and public policy questions; *Regulation*, a bimonthly journal examining all aspects of government regulation of society; and *AEI Economist*, a monthly newsletter analyzing current economic issues and evaluating future trends (or for all three publications, send an additional $12).

Call 202/862-7170 or write: AMERICAN ENTERPRISE INSTITUTE
1150 Seventeenth Street, N.W., Suite 301, Washington, D.C. 20036